ENGAGING WITH PERPETRATORS OF DOMESTIC VIOLENCE

ENGAGING WITH PERPETRATORS OF DOMESTIC VIOLENCE

Practical Techniques for Early Intervention

KATE IWI AND CHRIS NEWMAN

Jessica Kingsley *Publishers*
London and Philadelphia

Task Sheet 2.1.1 on pages 45–8 is reproduced from Calvin
Bell with kind permission from Safer Families/Ahimsa.

The Risk Indicator Checklist on pages 55–7 is reproduced
from CAADA with kind permission.

Information Sheet 3.6.1 on p.143 is reproduced
with kind permission from DVIP.

First published in 2015
by Jessica Kingsley Publishers
73 Collier Street
London N1 9BE, UK
and
400 Market Street, Suite 400
Philadelphia, PA 19106, USA

www.jkp.com

Library of Congress Cataloging in Publication Data
A CIP catalog record for this book is available from the Library of Congress

British Library Cataloguing in Publication Data
A CIP catalogue record for this book is available from the British Library

ISBN 978 1 84905 380 8
eISBN 978 0 85700 7384

Printed and bound in Great Britain

CONTENTS

3 – INTERVENTIONS

4 – WHAT NEXT?

1 – INTRODUCTION

CHAPTER 1.1

Contextualising the Model

Child protection social workers and family support workers can today complete their training without learning a single thing about how to work with domestic violence perpetrators. Yet in case after case they are expected to do just that. This peculiar situation has arisen in part due to a controversy in the domestic violence (DV)[1] field surrounding skilling up frontline professionals to work with perpetrators. The arguments on each side look something like this:

---

1   Domestic violence is not just physical violence; the term as currently used refers to a pattern of coercive and controlling behaviour that takes place within an intimate relationship. This can range from severe and repeated physical violence through to persistent emotional and psychological abuse and financial control. Some people use the term 'domestic abuse' to refer to the same phenomenon, while others call it intimate partner violence (IPV).

Despite all this, the benefits of skilling frontline workers to do this work remain compelling: in the absence of any work with the perpetrator, the onus falls upon the woman to undergo assessment and ultimately to change. She is the one that social workers and other professionals feel frustrated with and sometimes accusatory towards. She *becomes* the problem and is seen as 'failing to protect'. Working with the perpetrator places the emphasis to change back on the person causing the problem.

But perhaps most importantly, a well-timed and well-placed intervention might genuinely make some people less risky and their children and (ex-)partners safer.

This book is primarily aimed at frontline practitioners like child protection social workers who want to engage with someone they suspect has been abusing an intimate partner. The exercises and techniques this handbook offers are aimed at helping them make the most of their limited client contact.

This handbook is *not* going to provide practitioners with a whole DV perpetrator programme. Accredited perpetrator programmes are long (24 weeks and upwards) and the research suggests that the resultant changes are deeper and more sustainable. There are lots of excellent perpetrator programmes out there – at the back of this book we provide the details of Respect, a UK-based organisation whose role it is to signpost practitioners and abusers to what's on offer, both in terms of models and UK services. We are aware that recent changes to the England and Wales child protection system have set a strict 26-week deadline for care proceedings to finish. This is because delays to decision-making can have an adverse effect on outcomes for children. This change to the system also creates implicit pressure for 'quick fix' interventions. Of course, pressure for shorter (and cheaper) interventions is not limited to

England and Wales. Whilst it would be wonderful if we could find a brief intervention which reliably produced sustainable reductions in abuse and violence in the home, there is no evidence that such an intervention exists at the present time, and the exercises in this book are certainly not designed to serve that function though they can be used more positively, for 'treatment' to be tested out before proceedings start.

The other thing this book is *not* is a guide to anger management, though it includes a couple of anger management techniques. This book is firmly directed at work with abuse in intimate relationships – abuse that's usually about all sorts of expectations that people have of one another *because* they're in an intimate relationship. Additionally, this book is not about anger per se – which is just an emotion, and one the authors have no issue with – it's about abusive behaviour, which is a whole different ball game.

We very much hope that the techniques we are suggesting here will be delivered alongside some separate work with the victim of the abuse. That part of the intervention is probably going to be the best way to increase family safety. What's more, there's always a danger that work with the perpetrator can mean that the victim feels relieved and reassured, but this may be unwarranted. A lot of women get back with partners or cancel plans to leave for a refuge when their abuser promises to get help. It could be that the abuser being worked with will prove impervious to these techniques and so it's important to make sure that the victim is really clear that there's no guarantee of change. While somebody works with the abuser, somebody else (ideally not the same person – that can get complicated) has to be encouraging the victim to continue assessing and planning for the safety of herself and the children.

We're not going to say any more about this, nor try to explain how to do safety planning work and all the other techniques that might help victims of domestic abuse. That's another book altogether.

We came across a 'brief guide' the other day which was 260 pages long, and we weren't happy. We're assuming that those who bought this book were attracted to its brevity. This brevity has been achieved by being very clear as to what it will and won't include.

So let's just summarise that. This book will *not*:

- teach how to work more effectively with the victim of the abuse

- explain how to assess or work with children living with family violence

- provide a full perpetrator programme

- teach group work with perpetrators

- prepare workers for undertaking a risk assessment for care proceedings

- help significantly with any research or theory papers – it's not an 'academic' text.

What this book will include – and in fact all it offers – are a few key techniques for those who end up with just a few sessions with a DV perpetrator (between one and ten meetings) and want to learn to:

- briefly assess them

- prepare them to do a full perpetrator programme

- make the most effective possible interventions to decrease the risk in the meantime.

The authors of this book have a combined total of 40 years' experience of working with DV perpetrators. We've been training people to make frontline interventions for about half of that time, and now train around 500 practitioners a year. We've developed a sense of what's most effective, easiest to learn and realistically applicable for frontline practitioners who aren't specialist perpetrator workers. We haven't reinvented any wheels here – we've just picked out the most commonly used and effective ways of working, including approaches from motivational work, anger management, cognitive behaviour therapy and feminist models. These are:

- building a working alliance whilst tackling denial and minimisation
- assessment and risk
- signals, time outs and safety plans
- extending the definition of violence and abuse
  - violence
  - emotional abuse and intimidation
  - abusing cultural privilege
  - sexual abuse
  - jealousy
  - using the children
- analysing incidents of abuse
- working on the impacts of abuse
- conflict resolution
- referring out.

We hope it helps.

Kate Iwi and Chris Newman have been working with domestic abusers in the UK for 20 years. To find out more about the training and consultancy they can provide go to www.fsa.me.uk, or contact them at chris@fsa.me.uk or iwikate@gmail.com

CHAPTER 1.2

Theoretical Influences

Primary theoretical models

A pluralist analysis of power

The most common mode of intervention for domestic violence offenders tends to combine two primary theoretical models. First, the feminist approach to domestic violence, which is based on the idea that domestic violence is a misuse of power and control, and is rooted in traditions that encourage men to believe that they are entitled to authority over their partners. From this perspective, men's violence is defined as learned and intentional behaviour rather than the consequence of individual pathology, stress, substance use or a 'dysfunctional' relationship. Group work based on this approach seeks to address domestic abuse through education and critical enquiry. The aim is to increase men's awareness of the distorting effects on their lives of gender role socialisation and encourage relationships based on autonomy and respect (Pence and Paymar 1993).

If you are delivering perpetrator work in Bangladesh, Papua New Guinea or the Democratic Republic of Congo you'll need to focus on these traditional gendered inequalities because they are still the overwhelming reason for domestic violence. Over the past 20 years in the UK, however, we have seen a change in the shape of domestic violence cases coming to the attention of the family courts. We've moved from having more homogeneous caseloads of men abusing patriarchy to abuse in more diverse and complex relationships where all sorts of power axes intercept (e.g. race, age, nationality). In this book we have therefore replaced the simple feminist 'power and control wheel' with a more pluralist flexible approach which allows the practitioner to identify whether and which kinds of power, privilege, status and authority might be being abused in a given case. Chapter 3.4 covers a wide range of possibilities but is by no means exhaustive. For instance, one man's abuse may be rooted in gender-based entitlement in easily recognised and traditional ways, while in another case an abusive woman may mobilise similar ideas about masculinity to make her male partner feel emasculated at the thought of reporting her abuse of him. A pluralist perspective (Robert A. Dahl and Seymour Martin Lipset) allows the practitioner to put aside assumptions and analyse power from outcomes – Who is, in fact, living in fear? Who does seem to have control of the other? Who gets hurt? – and then to work backwards to consider how such effects have been achieved.

Cognitive behaviour therapy

The other primary theory of change underpinning perpetrator programmes is the cognitive behavioural approach. This approach – developed out of the cognitive therapy of Aaron Beck and the rational emotive therapy of Albert Ellis – works on the basis that changing maladaptive thinking leads to change in affect and ultimately in behaviour.

Cognitive behaviour therapy (CBT) aims to help the client to identify and adjust the thought patterns, assumptions, expectations and beliefs which contribute to the use of violence and abuse. Behavioural analysis is also used to identify the function of the problem behaviour in the person's life. Interventions are tailored to gently question and deconstruct these thoughts and beliefs.

The CBT approach fits well with a pluralist analysis of power and control since it too begins from an agnostic stance and enables the practitioner and client to begin with an incident of abuse and dig down to identify what must have been the underlying and driving beliefs for their behaviour. As a result, the approach is effective for men's violence to women partners, women's violence to male partners and for those who are abusive in same sex relationships. A critical overview of the research on alternative approaches (Gondolf 2011) shows that there is weak or insufficient supporting evidence for them at present. There is strong generic evidence for the use of the cognitive behavioural approach in batterer programmes. Gondolf believes that a greater focus on system implementation rather than alternative treatment methods would give rise to improved outcomes.

Other models

In our value base and general stance towards the work, we have been strongly influenced by the 'invitational' approach advocated by Alan Jenkins (2009) and the 'good lives model' developed by Tony Ward and colleauges (2007). These authors move beyond targeting specific problem behaviours and advocate a more holistic approach, helping clients to identify values, ethical commitments and life goals, and to understand how abuse in relationships impairs these goals. Part 2 of this handbook, which focuses on engagement and assessment, is influenced by these authors as well as Miller and Rollnick's (2002) work on motivational interviewing.

A multi-theoretical approach

In practice, few programmes in current use actually restrict themselves to one approach. As Babcock (2002, p.1026) points out:

> To the extent that CBT groups address patriarchal attitudes, and Duluth model groups address the learned and reinforced aspects of violence, any distinction between CBT and Duluth model groups becomes increasingly unclear.

Most programmes also contain some educational and experiential exercises aimed at increasing empathy for victims and increasing awareness of impacts on children. While some interventions strive to shape the programme to the needs of particular 'typologies' of perpetrator, we have resisted this and again preferred approaches that allow the worker to set out 'agnostic' as to typology of abuser just as much as reason for abuse.

> In our previous research of the men who drop out and repeatedly reassault their partners, no one psychological or relational profile stood out, and they didn't appear to fit into any of the prescribed categories of the alternative approaches. (Gondolf and White 2001)

References

Gondolf, E.W. (2011) 'The weak evidence for batterer program alternatives.' *Aggression and Violent Behavior 16*, 347–353.

Gondolf, E., and White, R. (2001) 'Batterer Program Participants Who Repeatedly Reassault: Psychopathic Tendencies and Other Disorders.' *Journal of Interpersonal Violence, 16*, 361–380

Jenkins, A. (2009) *Becoming Ethical: A Parallel Political Journey with Men Who Have Abused*. Lyme Regis: Russell House Publishing.

Miller, W.S. and Rollnick, S. (2002) *Motivational Interviewing*. New York: Guilford Press.

Pence, E. and Paymar, M. (1993) *Education Groups for Men Who Batter: The Duluth Model*. New York: Springer Publishing.

Ward, T., Mann, R.E. and Gannon, T.A. (2007) 'The good lives model of offender rehabilitation: Clinical implications.' *Aggression and Violent Behavior 12*, 87–107.

Further reading

Babcock, J., Green, C., and Robie, C. (2002) 'Does batterer treatment work? A meta-analytic review of domestic violence.' *Clinical Psychological Review, 8*, 1023–53.

Dutton, D. (1998) *The Abusive Personality: Violence and Control in Intimate Relationships*. New York: Guilford Press.

Dutton, D. and Corvo, K. (2006) 'Transforming a flawed policy: A call to revive psychology and science in domestic violence research and practice.' *Aggression and Violent Behavior 11*, 457–483.

Hamel, J. (2010) 'Do we want to be politically correct, or do we want to reduce partner violence in our communities?' *Partner Abuse 1*, 82–91.

Healey, K., Smith, S. and O'Sullivan, C. (1998) *Batterer Intervention: Program Approaches and Criminal Justice Strategies*. Washington, DC: US Department of Justice Office of Justice Programs, National Institute of Justice.

Holtzworth-Munroe, A. and Meehan, J. (2004) 'Typologies of men who are maritally violent: Scientific and clinical implications.' *Journal of Interpersonal Violence 19*, 1369–1389.

Rosenberg, M. (2003) *Nonviolent Communication: A Language of Life*, 2nd edition. Encinatas, CA: PuddleDancer Press.

Yee Lee, M., Sebold, J. and Uken, A. (2003) *Solution-Focused Treatment of Domestic Violence Offenders: Accountability for Change*. Oxford: Oxford University Press.

2 – ASSESSMENT AND ENGAGEMENT

CHAPTER 2.1

Assessment Interview

Making the connection

So let's continue with the presumption that you're a child protection social worker and you contact a father who you suspect of using violence to the mother. It's quite likely that he'll be hard to find and may be unresponsive to your initial letter or call. Before you give up, ask yourself, how hard have you tried to reach him? If he were the mother, what more would you do in order to get a meeting with him?

Dads can be harder to reach, but workers are often also less tenacious in their efforts to meet up with them. Perhaps we're secretly hoping that we can make a couple of attempts and then give up – with the thought that our jobs will be easier, less scary and more familiar if we only have to work with mums and children.

Stance

If you do manage to set up a meeting with a suspected abuser, male or female, you've already really achieved something. Whether they engage or not, you're going to learn something about the family that will help your work overall. A significant factor in how useful your engagement will be from here will depend on your *stance*. In particular, there's a tension when working with those who we think have behaved abusively, a tension between colluding with them on the one hand and becoming accusatory on the other – often in an over-zealous attempt to avoid collusion. Somewhere between the collusive and the accusatory stance lies a more neutral position, which is generally more constructive. Table 2.1 might give you a better idea about how these different approaches feel and the client–worker relationships they foster.

It's important that you make professional judgements about your client's abusive behaviour – it is an essential part of your job to assess the harm that has been caused and that might be caused in the future. It's human that you'll make personal judgements and have emotional reactions about some of the things you hear. However, it's also important that you form an alliance with your client towards change.

Change will come about when the internal conflict or dissonance within a person becomes unsustainable for them. To allow this to happen your job will be to help to build up the part of your client that wants a better life, the part with whom the violence and abuse don't fit well, the part that cares about their family, the part that would feel terrible if anyone else did that to them. If the person you are working with starts to feel judged and criticised, or picks up on your reactions to their behaviour, they are likely to become defensive. Then the conflict will end up being between you; you'll do all the urging to change while he sits back and gets more and more entrenched and invested in staying put.

On the other hand, if you find yourself avoiding the difficult challenges, overemphasising your relationship and becoming essentially client-centred, your client will happily use the time with you to get support without working significantly on their violence and abuse at all.

Table 2.11: Different stances and the client-worker relationship they foster

Collusive stance	Neutral stance	Accusatory stance
Getting matey – an alliance forms	Alliance forms with the side of him that wants to change	There is opposition rather than alliance forms
Session feels warm throughout	The sessions are difficult because the client experiences internal conflict and vulnerable feelings	The sessions feel difficult due to conflict between the worker and client, and the client primarily feels angry
There is little challenge or conflict	You make gentle but persistent invitations to him to challenge himself	There is a high level of challenge
You sit alongside him to look at others' behaviour	You sit alongside him to look at his abusive behaviour	You confront him with his wrongdoing
You empathise when he speaks of himself as a victim of others	You empathise when he seems to feel badly about his abuse	You don't empathise at all
A lot of time is spent trying to look at other people's behaviour and its impact on him	Most of the time is spent looking at his abusive behaviour and the impact on others	Most of the time is spent with you trying to tell your client how bad and impactful his behaviour is and with him defending himself
The session is non-judgemental	You leave space and invite him to make judgements about his own behaviour and then empathise with how hard that is	You let him know your judgements – both professional and personal – about his behaviour
He may comment on or feel how much more understanding you are than his partner	He may come to value and respect your help	He dislikes you and may put you down

We want to begin this book by encouraging you to practise taking a neutral stance with your client. We want to emphasise the idea of stance or manner because we're not suggesting you suspend any judgement or agenda internally – both intuitive judgement and the law of the land indicate that violence in intimate relationships is unacceptable. However, we recommend that you put your feelings and reactions aside in the session unless you're sure they're conducive to change in your client. Be curious and interested and share that interest with your client; try to use the 'Columbo approach' where you can and invite them to question their own behaviour as far as possible, but be calm and non-conflictual.

With that in mind, we will go on to describe approaches that should allow your early meetings to yield the kind of information that will help you decide if you can work with this person, and think about what other interventions will make this family safer.

Stages in working with a domestic violence perpetrator

Essentially there are two distinct steps to working with perpetrators. It will help you a great deal to delineate these in your own mind as clearly as possible:

1. *finding out* what has happened and assessing risk

2. *intervention*: assessing suitability for intervention and then working for change alongside the person you are working with.

If you try to mix step 2 into step 1, you may well find that you fail on both fronts. For example, if you're just hearing about the build-up to an abusive incident and you start asking, 'What do you think that was like for your partner and children?', you may make your client defensive, which means they're likely to retreat from any openness they might have had in their account of the incident.

We advise you to go easy on yourself and on them; set out in your first session or two simply to get an account of what has been happening. Towards the end of one of these sessions you might be able to make a light-touch intervention (which we'll cover below) that may nonetheless be quite powerful. You might also neutrally summarise and reflect back some of the abuse and violence they've told you about here and there during the session. Trust that telling another person even a bit of what you have done and then hearing it reflected back, without any blame, judgement or justifications, is an intervention in and of itself.

Setting out

Professionals often ask people for their understanding of what the meeting is about. It's a useful way to ascertain whether there are misconceptions that need clarifying. It's also worth adding something to acknowledge the difficulty of the subjects you are going to cover:

> *How were you feeling about coming in today? I would guess this wasn't a meeting you were looking forward to. What made you think it mattered enough to come along despite that?*

This might allow the client to give you some idea of their better side; to tell you that they care about their children, their partner or their family more generally.

They may immediately start to tell you about their experience of other professionals and 'the system' or you might ask them a bit about this. The stories people tell you about other professionals they've been involved with frequently carry useful information about how you can best work with them and/or provide a glimpse of how they might be talking about you six months down the line.

Remember your neutral stance – you can 'reposition' your client's anger as you go by reflecting back the values that are implicit, even in angry and blaming statements:

You feel like no one has heard your side...

- *... so being listened to is really important to you*

- *... so fairness really matters to you*

- *... so justice is something you feel really strongly about – tell me what you mean by justice.*

Explaining your role

At some point you should clarify your role – whatever that may be – for example:

As you may know there have been concerns about your child/ren in relation to [e.g. some police callouts to your home]. It's my job to find out whether these are concerns you're willing and able to engage with and whether we can work together to ensure the children are safe, happy and well.

Note that we would avoid saying, 'I'm here to get your version of events', since this seems to be an invitation to deny and minimise. If you really feel you have to say something along these lines, try:

I'm interested in how you see these incidents – because that tells me a lot about how you are going to keep your children safe in future. A rule of thumb is that social workers worry less when the parents worry more. If I think you're taking the concerns seriously that will be reassuring to me.

Getting consent to ask direct questions

A next step is to get consent to ask the many and intrusive questions that will form the body of your interview. It takes a minute or two to set this up well and it is worth doing.

> *I need to ask you some very direct questions about these issues – is that OK? But let me know if I ask you something you don't want to answer – would you speak out?*

or

> *We have only just met and I might need to ask some difficult questions. If you start to feel annoyed or uncomfortable, how could you let me know you want to take a five-minute break instead of walking out or having a go at me?*

You can't make anyone talk to you about things they don't want to talk about, so you may as well build in safe 'get-outs' for them. In a similar vein, it may help to say early on:

> *A lot of people find they remember more details as they go along – sometimes weeks later.*

This leaves a 'back door' for the client to disclose more as time goes on – whether that's due to increasing pressures from the court system or to your interventions with them.

Finding out about the violence and abuse

Do chat a little about the early stages of the relationship, but don't spend so long that an anxious sense of 'beating about the bush' develops. This person knows what you are here to discuss and so it can be almost reassuring if you move quite soon towards talking about the abuse. Some key pointers that will help guide you are as follows.

DON'T GET STUCK WITH GENERAL QUESTIONS

If you ask general questions, you'll get vague, evasive and often 'idealising' answers. Questions like 'How is your relationship?' become richer and more useful if you add, 'What are the best and worst aspects of it?' And even those kinds of questions will yield more vivid information if you ask, 'Can you give me a specific example of that (the best and worst aspects) or tell me a story about something that would illustrate that aspect of the relationship?'

AVOID YES/NO QUESTIONS

Questions such as 'Don't you think that would have upset her?' or 'So did you hit her just the once?' often imply a right and a wrong answer that will make your client feel trapped or offer them an easy get-out.

AVOID 'WHY?'

The only time to ask why is if you are genuinely exploring something – in which case phrases like 'Can you explain …?' or 'Can you help me to understand …' might be preferable. 'Why?' can sound judgemental, and this will only push your client onto the defensive and wake up the part of them that wants to justify and minimise what they did. Remember your neutral stance.

TALK TO WHERE THEY ARE AT

Speak in language that fits this person's current experience. They are unlikely to relate to being called a domestic violence perpetrator just now, so asking when they first used domestic violence won't help. Asking about the very first time they got physical with a partner when arguing might be easier for them to relate to.

GET BEYOND THE CASE RECORDS

While the things you know about can be a convenient place to start, try to free yourself from acting and talking as if the events in the 'chronology' or the 'index offence' are the only times they've been abusive. Statistically speaking, that's highly unlikely to be the case.

USE A SCHEDULE PURELY AS AN AIDE MEMOIRE

Below is an 'interview schedule' of some of the kinds of questions that might help you – consider them a reminder rather than a script. If you really just sit and ask a long string of questions you will find that you have more of an interrogation on your hands than an interview.

Violence in the relationship

- *When and how did you two first meet?*

- *I assume that the relationship worked well at first – what do you think worked best about you two?*

- *What issues did you argue over at first? And later?*

- *When did you first get worried about how you deal with anger?*

- *When did you first lay a hand on your partner in anger?*

- *Tell me about some other times when you've gone too far. Or when you haven't used the right methods to stand up for yourself.*

- *What are you like these days when you are angry? At your best and at your worst? Can you give me recent examples of each?*

- *How do you get physical with your partner when arguing? Let's consider a particular time – if you could see a film of yourself during that argument, how would you look? Did you pace around, shout, bang things, break things, stand close to her when shouting, etc.?*

- *How long do arguments last? How do they end?*

- *How often do arguments like this happen?*

- *What do you feel is the worst thing you've done to your partner? What would your partner say is the worst thing?*

- *What is the most recent thing you've done?*

- *Have you ever got her to do sexual things that retrospectively you think she was uncomfortable about? How did you get her to do that?*

- *Tell me about your earlier relationships and in what ways they were similar to and different from this.*

- *Have the police been called in the past? How many times?*

- *Any social services involvement?*

Parenting

- *Tell me a bit about each of your children.*

- *What makes you proud of them?*

- *What things do they struggle with more than other kids of their age?*

- *How did you hope being a parent would be?*

- *What's working?*

- *What are the best times for you as a parent?*

- *What are the hardest times for you?*

- *How has the violence in your relationship affected your relationship with your children?*

- *What do you think they are aware of?*

- *What have you noticed about how the children are affected by the violence and abuse between the adults?*

- *Do you talk with your children about the violence and conflict in the family? What do you say? What would you want to say, if you could?*

- *Is there anyone else the children talk to about this? Who else is important to them?*

- *What do you find hardest about each child's behaviour? Tell me about a time when your children have misbehaved. Why do you think they act like that?*

- *How do you try to manage that – at your best and when you're at your worst? What kinds of discipline do you use? What happens if this doesn't work? Do the kids sometimes get smacked? Do you and the children's mother agree about how to discipline them?*

- *Did they see the violence?* (If he says they were not in same room, ask where they were in the house.)

- *How do you think seeing the violence affected the kids? If they weren't in the room, how would they have felt listening to what went on? Or seeing the after-effects?* (Ask if there were injuries to their mother or damaged property. Would the children have seen this?)

- *What do you think the effect of growing up seeing Dad hit/insult/shout at Mum is on the children?*

Childhood

- *What were things like between your parents or carers?*

- *Did you see or hear violence between them when you were a child?*

- *What was it like if they argued and fought?*

- *Did you ever get hurt yourself?*

- *Some people talk about being neglected or treated roughly as a child. Did anything like this happen to you?*

- *Who do you think was to blame for the violence?*

- *Did they ever get help?*

Returning to your own relationship and taking action

- *So you've been together X years and you've gone from [first bullying behaviour] to [worst bullying behaviour]. If the violence and abuse continued to escalate in the same manner, where would your relationship be another X years down the line?*

- *How do you want to be as a partner and father? Is it different from how you've been? In what way?*

- *How do you feel about coming in for [X sessions] with me [or elsewhere]? Do you feel able to commit to this?*

- *Have you tried doing a course before [on any subject]? If you didn't finish it or go regularly why was that?*

- *Have you ever said you'll change or won't do it again? Did you keep your word? What got in the way?*

USE INVENTORIES

After a verbal interview we really recommend using the inventories (see Task Sheet 2.1.1 at the end of this chapter). If your client is able to read and write then leave them with these for ten minutes, then come back and glance over them, asking about anything that leaps out at you. We find that some people are much more willing to disclose difficult information in a questionnaire than face to face.

Not only is it impossible that you remember to ask about every form of abuse, but letting someone alone with a list and their thoughts allows them time to reflect away from the scrutiny of the worker. This seems in some cases to effect less image management and thus increase disclosure. The inventories are useful for assessing 'two-way' violence in relationships, which is examined later in the chapter.

Working with denial and minimisation at the assessment stage

The most common problem that social workers face when attempting to address the issue of domestic violence is parents' unwillingness to speak openly about what has been happening. If we want to create the best conditions possible for disclosure, it is important to put ourselves into the parents' shoes and understand the factors which make people want to cover up or deny when a professional makes enquiries about their family.

FEAR OF CONSEQUENCES

The most obvious factor which contributes to denial is the parents' fears about what the consequences will be if they do give a full account of what has been going on. Parents often say they covered up the abuse because they were afraid that their children would be taken away. They may fear that their family and community will find out what has happened and that they or their family will be ostracised or shamed. Perpetrators may additionally fear criminal prosecution or losing their job. These are powerful fears, and anyone who has them is likely to be very cautious about what they tell a professional.

While you cannot guarantee that these fears will not be realised, some may be highly exaggerated and unrealistic.

It is useful to guess at and explore worst fears – reassuring and minimising your client's worries where you can.

SHAME

Remember that when we start a conversation with someone about domestic abuse, we are asking a complete stranger to talk with us about some of the worst things they have ever done. In this kind of situation, some degree of justification, minimisation and externalisation of blame are normal. Most people will use these tactics when asked about something they feel badly about – they are a sign of inner conflict about the abuse, or at the very least of an awareness of social conventions. In light of this, the absence of any attempt to justify or minimise the abuse would probably be a worrying sign (indeed some research shows that those perpetrators who fail to deny their actions at the time of arrest are actually more likely to offend again, e.g. Henning and Holdford 2006).

Shame will make it less likely that a person will want to disclose what they have done and more likely that they will interpret you as being judgemental of them. People who feel bad about themselves are often hyper-alert to signs of criticism, so you'll need to manage your own emotional reactions to hearing about abuse.

If you hear your client minimise their abuse or tell nasty stories about why the victim deserved it, therefore, take a breath and remember:

- You are gaining information about your client's world view, their thinking patterns, their insight into their abuse and their levels of hostility towards their partner.

- Dealing with denial, minimisation of the abuse, partner-blame and other justifications are the bread and butter of this work. Regard increased disclosure as a goal of the work, rather than a prerequisite.

MINIMISATION

Minimisation is when we make the abuse or its impact seem less serious, less pervasive or less recent. Professionals often hear that the violence only happened 'once or twice', 'We have arguments, like any couple', or that all that's happened are the few incidents that have made it onto public record.

While 'Tell me what happened' might be a useful opener, you'll quickly find that such open questions can lead you way off your agenda. We don't want to script you or suggest you say things that don't sound like 'your own voice', but we do advise that you choose the wording of questions carefully depending on the kinds of response you're after. Your questions need to be open enough to get your client talking, but they need to be directive enough to maintain a focus on his or her behaviour – not about what their partner or anyone else did. Get used to asking, 'What did you do next?', and to repeating this in different ways until you've got the picture. This means using a style of interviewing you might associate more with the police when they are trying to piece together a detailed account of an incident.

To get a brief, simple idea of risk and to glean some information for future interventions, you will want to find out as far as possible about the first, the worst and the most recent incidents of violence. If you have more time you can track the spaces between in more detail afterwards.

You will want to form a clear picture of each incident, starting from when the argument began and running through the perpetrator's actions step by step up until the violence came to a stop. Get into details: Where were they – he and she and the children – when the argument began? At what point did they move from A to B? What was the abuser saying? On a scale of 1 to 10, how loudly? How and where did they first touch their partner? How hard? What did they do next? And so on.

You might find the process gets awkward or that your client gets defensive. If they do, then acknowledge and discuss the barriers to disclosure by saying something like:

> *I can see this is difficult to talk about – I am a relative stranger and this is clearly stuff that doesn't fit with how you want to be as a father and husband. I guess you may want to reassure me that you're OK. Sometimes people assume that if they deny any problems I'll be reassured. Actually I am most reassured by a degree of disclosure and a willingness to work with me to change. When I feel I've reason to worry but am faced with blanket denial, I worry more.*

Perhaps the most important technique, though, is to be neutrally persistent in order to get the detail and context of what happened. When you feel you have gone off track, gently guide your client back to the details of what happened:

> *Earlier on I asked how your partner got those injuries and I'm afraid I still don't have a clear picture of how. I know it's difficult to talk about but I'm going to take you back.*

It can be helpful to switch into a present tense account to help the parent get back into the thoughts and feelings at the time:

> *So, you're both in the kitchen and you've just said '...' and she's just said '...' and then what do you do next?*

When exploring the frequency and severity of abusive behaviour, try using scales – for instance:

> *On a scale of 1 to 5 (with 5 being punching her as hard as you can) how hard did you punch her?*

Ask for details of the words that the abuser used – ask for exactly what was said and how:

> *On a scale of 1 to 5, where 5 is as loudly as you can possibly shout, how loudly were you shouting and what did you shout?*

And a final tip, pitch your questions about the violence at higher levels than you would guess has been used – this makes it easier for your client to disclose the real level of violence:

> *Worker: So how many times did you hit her? Are we talking like an onslaught? 30 or 40 times?*
>
> *Client: Good God no! It was only a couple of times.*
>
> *Worker: Like four or five times?*
>
> *Client: No, like three times.*

Whereas if you simply ask, 'Did you hit her the once?', the answer is very likely just to be a yes.

PARTNER BLAME

It is almost inevitable that the person you are interviewing will try to pass blame for their actions over to their partner by telling you what she did to deserve it.

It's really tempting, when you hear a hostile allegation about the victim of the abuse, to want to jump to their defence. ('How much does she actually drink?', 'Maybe she wasn't kissing this other guy in that way?', etc.) Beware. Hold fast to the idea that violence is wrong even if one has an alcoholic, unfaithful, provocative or otherwise unpleasant partner. Given this, whether the allegations about his or her partner are true or not is irrelevant to your assessment of the risk the abuser poses. Don't even imply that it is relevant by spending effort arguing over such allegations. Work simply on this basis:

> *I don't know your partner or her side of things – but let's assume that she will continue to be exactly as she always has, and let's focus on how you've responded – and later we'll think about how you could respond differently in future.*

There are also some speedy ways to avoid colluding without getting too drawn into the issue of who is to blame. The most obvious is reframing. For example:

> *Client: She was screaming hysterically at me.*
>
> *Worker: So, she was really angry with you. What did you do next?*

Where partner blame is pervasive, you might want to explicitly seek your client's consent to interrupt and shut it down.

> *Your partner isn't here. Nothing that you and I can do in this room is going to change her. The only person you can change is you. So let's think together about what you did and how you might have handled the situation differently. To keep you focused on that I am going to interrupt and bring you back to talking about yourself when you seem to be focusing a lot on your partner – is that OK?*

Assessing 'two-way' violence in relationships

There is a lot of controversy in the research literature about the prevalence of female-to-male domestic violence (for a good summary of the research see Johnson 2008).[1] The puzzle arises from the fact that whilst surveys in the general population indicate that men and women use some form of violence in relationships at roughly equal rates, this does not fit with the experience of those working in frontline agencies such as the police, probation and children's services, where there is a significant majority of male perpetrators.

Johnson believes that this mismatch is caused because domestic violence is a complex phenomenon, where there are different patterns of violence, different motivations for the violence and different power dynamics within

---

1   Johnson identified five types of domestic violence based on the motivation of the perpetrator, the pattern of violence and the power dynamic within the relationship:

1. 'Coercive-controlling violence', or 'intimate terrorism', involves the use (in heterosexual relationships, usually by men) of multiple tactics of coercion and (usually, but not always) physical violence, in an attempt to achieve and maintain general control over a partner and access to domestic, emotional and sexual services.

2. 'Violent resistance' involves a woman employing self-defensive, retaliatory or pre-emptive violence in response to 'battery' by her partner.

3. 'Situational couple violence' shows huge variability; it occurs in the context of isolated power struggles, jealousy or other incidents of conflict, and it involves one or both parties using verbal aggression and/or violence, usually (but by no means always) of a minor nature. According to Johnson, women initiate this kind of violence and are the sole or primary perpetrator as often as men.

4. 'Separation-instigated violence' occurs for the first time in the context of relationship breakdown and separation; the violence is usually, but by no means always, of a minor nature, and is perpetrated by men and women.

5. 'Mutual violent control' occurs when both partners employ coercive-controlling violence (only found in a small minority of couples).

the relationship. He believes that the most prevalent form of violent conflict among heterosexual couples (what he calls 'situational couple violence' – see footnote 1) shows few gender differences, and is usually minor in nature (although it can escalate into lethal conflict). However, the least common, but most severe, form of domestic violence (coercive control) is committed predominantly by men – and importantly this form of violence is much more common in referrals to statutory agencies and emergency services.

To assess effectively and respond appropriately, especially with children's welfare in mind, we therefore need to get a detailed picture of the pattern of violence and abuse in the relationship – this means examining the role played by both partners and avoiding prior assumptions in our approach to an assessment. At the same time we need to be wary about falling into simplistic formulations such as 'they are just as bad as each other'.

We find the most useful way to deal with all this is to enquire in detail with both partners about the specific patterns of abuse in this and previous relationships. This means, on a case-by-case basis, looking in detail at both overall patterns of violence and abuse, and unpacking the dynamics of specific incidents, to get as much information as possible with each partner about:

- the frequency and severity of the full range of behaviours which fit within the definition of domestic abuse

- whether there are patterns of behaviour as opposed to isolated incidents; incidents of abuse that may not look severe in isolation will give rise to greater concerns if they fit within a wider pattern of abuse and domination

- who is physically stronger and who has the greater capacity for violence and to induce fear. Who is afraid of who?

- what the overall impact of the abuse has been on each partner

- whether one partner feels controlled in their day-to-day life (what they do, where they go, who they see, what they wear, etc.) by the other

- what effect it would have on the child to live in a home where this type of abuse is going on.

- The inventories we have provided in Task Sheet 2.1.1 will provide a helpful aid to this kind of assessment.

References

Henning, C. and Holdford, R. (2006) 'Minimization, denial, and victim blaming by batterers: How much does the truth matter?' *Criminal Justice and Behavior 33*, 110.

Johnson, M. (2008) *A Typology of Domestic Violence*. Boston, MA: Northeastern University Press.

TASK SHEET 2.1.1

Behaviour Inventories

Abuse					
Name:				Date:	
? Don't know	0 Never	1 Once	2 Occasionally	3 Frequently	4 Constantly
Score your-self here – *what I did*	**Instructions:** Using the scale above, place a score in each box in the left-hand column to indicate how often you have behaved towards your (ex-)partner in the way described. Then score them in the right-hand column. Delete or change any words that don't apply.				Score your part-ner here '– *what they did*
	Insulted them (such as calling them a hurtful name)				
	Humiliated them (made fun of them)				
	Told them that they were worthless or ugly				
	Told them that they were stupid or mad				
	Told them that they were a bad parent				
	Told them that no one else would put up with them				
	Told them that they wouldn't be able to cope on their own				
	Tried to stop them having contact with their friends or family				
	Insisted on accompanying them whenever they went out				
	Locked them in				
	Insisted on knowing who they were with at all times you were not together				

	Accused them unfairly of having sex with other people	
	Followed them or checked up on them when you were not together	
	Threatened to kill yourself if they left you	
	Threatened to report them to the police/social services/immigration if they left you	
	Threatened to kidnap the child/ren if they left you	
	Told them that you would never let them bring up the child/ren with another partner	
	Insisted they obey you or tried to control just about everything they did	
	Insisted they carry out housework to your standard	
	Forced them to cook meals that you chose	
	Forced them to wear clothes or make-up that you chose for them	
	Controlled the money (e.g. dictated how the family income was spent)	
	Put them on an 'allowance' or made them ask or beg for money	
	Made them account for every penny they spent	
	Made false allegations about them to the police/social services	
	Frightened them with your temper	
	Punched or kicked the door, wall or furniture	
	Stopped them using the phone to get help	
	Intentionally damaged their clothes, possessions or property	
	Swore and shouted in their face	
	Physically threw them out of the home	
	Smashed plates or threw food or objects around	
	Threatened them by raising your fist at them	
	Threatened them with an object	
	Threatened to kill them	

Violence					
? Don't know	0 Never	1 Once	2 Occasionally	3 Frequently	4 Constantly
Score your-self here – *what I did*	**Instructions:** Using the scale above, place a score in each box in the left-hand column to indicate how often you have behaved towards your (ex-)partner in the way described. Then score them in the right-hand column. Delete or change any words that don't apply.				Score your part-ner here – *what they did*
	Spat at them				
	Poked them with your finger				
	Pushed them				
	Dragged them by the clothes, arm, leg or hair (delete as necessary)				
	Held them by the arms or shoulders				
	Grabbed or shaken them (delete as necessary)				
	Pinned them up against the wall				
	Pulled their hair				
	Thrown them around				
	Twisted or bent their finger, arm or leg (delete as necessary)				
	Pinched, scratched or squeezed them (delete as necessary)				
	Bitten them				
	Poured or thrown a drink or other liquid over them (delete as necessary)				
	Thrown things at them that could hurt				
	Burnt them with a cigarette				
	Slapped them				

	Hit them with the back of your hand	
	Punched them to the arm, leg, body, head or face (delete as necessary)	
	Kicked them in the arm, leg, body, head or face (delete as necessary)	
	Banged their head	
	Head-butted them	
	Pushed them down the stairs	
	Smothered their mouth	
	Held them by the throat	
	Tried to choke or strangle them	
	Hit them with an object	
	Stabbed them	
	[Male partner only] Assaulted your partner when you knew she was pregnant	
	[Male partner only] Punched your partner in the abdomen when you knew she was pregnant	

Note: Inventories developed by and used with permission from Calvin Bell at Safer Families/Ahimsa.

CHAPTER 2.2

Risk Assessment

Whether or not your job involves making formal assessments of risk, the reality is that all of us who work with violence are constantly having to assess risk, often in rapidly changing situations, using incomplete and unreliable information. We know that if we overestimate risk, we may subject the family unnecessarily to disruptive and distressing interventions, whereas if we underestimate risk, we are likely to leave children and parents without the protection they need.

The best we can do in these circumstances is to take a careful and systematic approach to making judgements about risk. The following information will guide you towards focusing on the risk-relevant issues from the outset and help you to make your interviews with parents more productive.

Risk factors

If we want to make a defensible assessment of risk, it is essential to focus our enquiries on the presence or absence of factors which have been shown in research to be associated with increased risk of domestic violence recidivism.

History of violence

A key lesson here is to anchor the assessment in the person's past behaviour (static or historical factors), rather than relying too much on how they behave in interview. This is because research has repeatedly demonstrated that clinical impressions are the least reliable source of information about risk, and assessments based solely on such impressions are no better than chance at predicting whether someone is going to offend again (see, for instance, Hilton, Harris and Rice 2000).

As the most powerful predictor of future behaviour is past behaviour, we need to gather as much information as possible about the pattern of abuse in current and previous relationships (if there has been domestic violence in another relationship, this is a strong indicator the violence is likely to reoccur). Look in detail at:

- frequency and severity of physical assault
- the frequency, intensity and duration of emotional/psychological abuse, jealous and isolating behaviour, 'coercive control'[1]
- sexual abuse within the relationship
- harassment during periods of separation.

Both parents may have quite restrictive definitions of 'violence', so it can be very helpful to use checklists or a list of questions about specific abusive behaviours (see Task Sheet 2.1.1 in Chapter 2.1).

---

1   Coercive control involves a pattern of violent, coercive and controlling behaviours which have the cumulative effect of depriving the victim of freedom in everyday life. The perpetrator uses such behaviour to secure privileges and services from the victim, via the 'micro-management of everyday behaviours' (see Stark 2007).

Other historical factors

There is a range of other historical factors which research has shown to be predictive of more serious domestic violence and which therefore warrant investigation and consideration:

- developmental history – in particular a history of maltreatment in childhood, exposure to violence in childhood and significant conduct/adjustment problems as a child

- substance use problems

- mental health problems

- general aggression

- a history of the child maltreating children

- criminal history (non-violent)

- perpetrator's failure to protect the child by exposing them to domestic violence

- a history of abuse by extended family members

- a low level of willingness to accept the decisions of the victim and the courts

- a history of employment problems.

Dynamic or changeable factors

In your interviews you will also be able to make an assessment of the attitudes, beliefs and thinking patterns that underlie the person's behaviour. Chapter 3.5 will help you to do this in more detail.

Does denial increase risk?

As we said previously, in the early stages of any kind of investigation, it is most likely that the suspected perpetrator will deny the seriousness of the concerns, blame their partner or other circumstances for whatever of their behaviour has become 'exposed' and often feel anger and outrage at you and at the system for exaggerating the risk they pose. Levels of disclosure will depend significantly on how the parent calculates the costs and benefits of coming clean at any given time.

Our advice is to make an assessment of risk based primarily on the information from other sources – especially about historical factors – whilst remaining aware that reduction in denial and an increase in motivation to change are *targets of intervention* more than they are significant risk prediction factors. As such, they are unlikely to be present at the outset.

Making clear statements about risk

Statements about risk need to be clear and closely specified and should include an estimation of:

1. **the likelihood …**

   e.g. unlikely to occur, may occur, is likely to occur, is very likely to occur

2. **of what kind of harm …**

   e.g. emotional abuse, physical violence

3. **to whom …**

   the adult partner? the children?

4. **at what level of frequency and severity …**

this estimate will be largely based on the kind of abuse the perpetrator has used in the past, but will also take into account potential escalation.

5. **within what timescale …**

    imminent risk? ongoing risk if nothing changes?

6. **and in what context?**

    when the couple are living together/apart? at time of threat to the relationship? at contact handover? if he finds out where she lives?

For instance:

> In my opinion, if the couple continue to live together, Mr X poses a substantial risk of using severe physical violence towards Ms Y and it is very likely that he will continue to use persistent and severe verbal aggression as well as emotional and psychological abuse towards Ms Y. I believe that the risk of physical violence will rise if Mr X returns to drinking at excessive levels, and if he feels the relationship with Ms Y is under threat.
>
> I believe that whilst the likelihood of direct abuse of the children is low, the possibility that they will be indirectly harmed during incidents cannot be discounted. Given their young age there is also a very high likelihood that they will be exposed to any abuse of their mother that takes place and this is likely to be traumatic and harmful to them.

In another case you might conclude that a perpetrator poses a low risk of committing physical violence, but a high risk of persistent and demeaning emotional abuse towards their partner.

It is also necessary to acknowledge factual uncertainties (also see 'weighting credibility' below) – for instance:

If Ms P's account is taken as the basis for estimating risk, this would indicate that Mr Q currently poses a high risk of severe (and potentially life-threatening) violence to her. His reported willingness to assault the mother while she was holding the child would also indicate that unless protective measures are taken the child will be at risk of exposure to severe domestic violence in the future.

Mr Q adamantly denies any violent behaviour and it is for the courts to decide on factual issues. However, given the seriousness of Ms P's allegations, I believe that they will need to be taken very seriously when planning for her and the child's safety, at least until the circumstances of the recent assault can be fully investigated.

Sharing the responsibility for high-risk cases

In the UK, it is currently recommended that a multidisciplinary response should be triggered when there are 14 or more 'yes' answers to 24 questions in the Risk Identification Checklist (RIC) (otherwise known as the CAADA-DASH[2]) or when professional judgement causes the referrer to raise the risk level for other reasons. At that point cases should be referred to the local MARAC (multiagency risk assessment conference) which can usually be located via the local police station. This ensures you will not be holding the case 'alone'. Whatever your assessment of the risk, it can change quickly, and we would strongly advise

---

2   CAADA (Co-ordinated Action against Domestic Abuse) is a national charity that works across the UK. DASH stands for domestic abuse, stalking and 'honour'-based violence.

that you do not work with domestic violence cases unless you have sound, 'risk aware' supervision or case management systems in place, and are in good communication with the professional network around you.

The RIC is provided below

Risk Indicator Checklist

This list is included for reference only; detailed guidance on how to use this assessment is available from www.caada.org.uk.

1. Has the current incident resulted in injury? [Please state what and whether this is the first injury.]

2. Is the victim very frightened?

3. What is the victim afraid of? Is it further injury or violence? [Please give an indication of what the victim thinks [name of abuser[s]...] might do and to whom, including children].

4. Does the victim feel isolated from family/friends, i.e. does [name of abuser[s]...] try to stop the victim from seeing friends/family/doctor or others?

5. Is the victim feeling depressed or having suicidal thoughts?

6. Has the victim separated or tried to separate from [name of abuser[s]...] within the past year?

7. Is there conflict over child contact?

8. Does [...] constantly text, call, contact, follow, stalk or harass the victim? [Please expand to identify what and whether the victim believes that this is done deliberately to intimidate the victim. Consider the context and behaviour of what is being done.]

9. Is the victim pregnant or has the victim recently had a baby [within the last 18 months]?

10. Is the abuse happening more often?

11. Is the abuse getting worse?

12. Does [...] try to control everything the victim does and/or are they excessively jealous? [In terms of relationships, who the victim sees, being 'policed at home' and telling the victim what to wear, for example. Consider 'honour'-based violence and specify behaviour.]

13. Has [...] ever used weapons or objects to hurt the victim?

14. Has [...] ever threatened to kill the victim or someone else and the victim believed them? [If yes, please identify who: the victim/children/other [please specify].

15. Has [...] ever attempted to strangle/choke/ suffocate/drown the victim?

16. Does [...] do or say things of a sexual nature that make the victim feel bad or that physically hurt the victim or someone else? [If someone else, specify who.]

17. Is there any other person who has threatened the victim or who the victim is afraid of? [If yes, please specify who and why. Consider extended family if 'honour'-based violence [HBV].]

18. Does the victim know if [...] has hurt anyone else? [Please specify whom including the children, siblings or elderly relatives. Consider HBV.]

19. Has [...] ever mistreated an animal or the family pet?

20. Are there any financial issues? For example, is the victim dependent on [...] for money/have they recently lost their job/other financial issues?

21. Has [...] had problems in the past year with drugs [prescription or other], alcohol or mental health leading to problems in leading a normal life? [If yes, please specify which and give relevant details if known.]

22. Has [...] ever threatened or attempted suicide?

23. Has [...] ever broken bail/an injunction and/or formal agreement for when they can see the victim and/or the children? [The victim may wish to consider this in relation to an ex-partner of the perpetrator if relevant.]

24. Does the victim know if [...] has ever been in trouble with the police or has a criminal history? [If yes, please specify whether DV, other violence or other.]

Weighing credibility

In cases which have moved into the court arena, it is the judge's role to decide on disputed facts. Therefore, where there are competing accounts, you may need to present different assessments of risk contingent on different versions of events. Thus you may need to say something like, 'The undisputed evidence indicates X level of risk. However, if the court finds Ms Y's account and that of her parents plausible, this would indicate a (much higher) level of risk.' Then outline in detail separate estimations of risk based on each of these scenarios.

Nevertheless, you may also be able to shed some light on the credibility of competing accounts, and if the case isn't in court then you'll have to decide for yourself which is more likely to be true. You may find that you just believe one version of events and it's likely that you're already (subconsciously) making such assessments on some of the following considerations. You'll need to ensure that your 'feeling' about what to believe is defensible, and that means building it on solid and absolutely conscious criteria such as:

- Which account is most consistent with that of other witnesses and testimony – especially non-partisan testimony such as medical and police records?

- It is likely that people will be motivated to exaggerate or minimise their versions of what occurred based on their calculations of the costs and benefits of doing so. It is reasonable to take this into account when weighing up the credibility of evidence from those who are partisan (e.g. children, parents, extended family).

- Does the person's behaviour in other settings suggest they are capable of the alleged behaviour?

- Was a given account told in a manner which was emotionally congruent?

- Is there inconsistency within a given person's account – within one interview and over time?

- Are they able to provide circumstantial detail?

- Logical consequence – does the account make sense? For instance, could the injuries logically have been caused in the way the client is stating? You don't have to be a medical expert to say how plausible a chain of events seems to you. This extends to being able to claim, for example, that, 'In my opinion, it is implausible that after three years of a happy marriage Ms X would have suddenly made such efforts to flee to a refuge.'

- Does the client express blanket positivity or negativity about the relationship – 'Everything was fine, we never argued'? In considering this you'll need to check definitions of key terms like 'argued', 'violence' and 'abuse' – someone may say their relationship is fine because they think of weekly arguments as normal and they may say they've never been violent to their partner because they think of violence as only involving acts like punching or kicking.

- Is there evidence of distorted thinking, which may lead to similarly distorted accounts?

Risk to workers

Lastly, it is important to remember that working with domestic violence can expose workers to physical risk, and we need to be demanding about our own safety. We owe it to ourselves, to our service users for whom we should model self-care, and to our children and significant others. The following points may help in setting up safe working practices.

- Ensure that you carry out risk interviews in a safe working environment with other adults around.

- Do not do challenging and exploratory work on home visits. Home visits are ideal for observation or for strength-building work but not for detailed interviews about violence with the perpetrator.

- Read chronologies and reports, before seeing service users, for indications of risk to professionals.

In cases where you are concerned about the risk to workers, discuss this with your line manager.

Fear is a very important indicator – don't be ashamed to come forward about it. Safeguards might include:

- choice of venue

- having a second person present

- explaining that you will be asking difficult direct questions and that you want to do so safely

- explaining that it isn't OK to shout, damage objects, or threaten or hurt you

- asking the service user how they can reassure you that they will not behave in such ways, even if they feel really frustrated with your questions

- agreeing to have a time out part way through an interview if needed

- having a panic button (you might agree with colleagues that if you press this they will knock on the door and say an urgent call has come in for you – giving you a chance to take some moments out and decide if other action is necessary)

- warning a fellow worker and having them on hand within earshot – again you might agree that if they hear raised voices they will disturb you on a pretext that allows you to leave the room momentarily and discuss whether any action is required.

- following your agency's security procedures – such as 'check-in' systems for the end of sessions

- checking whether your agency has a well-known and practised plan, in your local office, for what should happen if a worker sounds the panic alarm

- positioning yourself close to doors and panic buttons

- checking objects in the room and removing those that lend themselves easily to being used as weapons

- telling your supervisor when you find a client intimidating.

Often we feel foolish for feeling scared or learn to suppress our feelings in favour of appearing 'professional'. Don't allow yourself to do this. You owe it to those you work with and all those close to you to allow your organisation to take some responsibility for your safety.

You should also monitor the state of the interviewee and your own anxiety or fear levels. If you are getting worried about either of these, then you might try:

- explaining that these are 'standard' questions, which you ask of everybody

- acknowledging frustrations and discomforts

- changing the direction of your questioning

- suggesting a break or drawing the interview to a close.

References

Hilton, N.Z., Harris, G.T. and Rice, M.E. (2010) *Risk Assessment for Domestically Violent Men: Tools for Criminal Justice, Offender Intervention, and Victim Services.* Washington, DC: American Psychological Association.

Stark, E. (2007) *Coercive Control: How Men Entrap Women in Personal Life.* Oxford: Oxford University Press.

3 – INTERVENTIONS

As stated earlier, it's easiest and most effective if you separate the finding-out stage from the intervention stage. Even intervention is best done in some kind of order, generally from the more immediate and superficial/behavioural level, working gradually towards deeper attitudinal change. Some psychotherapeutic approaches might start right in the client's childhood and gently heal the deep hurts and then challenge the beliefs underlying the violence and the client's ability to tolerate vulnerability. When others are at risk, this kind of approach is simply too slow. Victims and children can't wait for someone to undergo this kind of therapeutic change. We therefore advocate beginning with the current behaviour and working backwards towards some of the self-talk. You probably won't get much further in your few short sessions – deconstructing deeply held belief systems will be beyond the scope of your time with this client and should be the stuff of specialist DV perpetrator programmes staffed by workers who have had substantial training in this area.

The rest of this book reflects this same ordering – prioritising the techniques which are likely to lead most directly to immediate improvements in the safety of victims and children.

Safety Plans, Signals and Time Outs

Assume from the outset that the person you're working with does not want to behave in a damaging and aggressive way. At a minimum you can be sure that they do not want any further involvement of statutory services in their lives. You can use this way of framing the problems to enlist them in some exploration of what happens in the build-up to their aggressive behaviour. Also, if you feel that a meeting with a client will leave them worried, angry or resentful at you or their partner, it is important to do some safety planning with them.

Safety planning

The aims when discussing safety planning with a potential perpetrator are actually much the same as for working with a victim. These are:

- to help them to anticipate and plan ahead, rather than reacting to events as they happen

- to prepare them to deal with crisis situations when they are at higher risk of being violent in ways that increase the (ex-)partner's and children's safety.

Here are some ways to invite your client into working with you on drawing up a safety plan:

- *Let's assume your partner isn't going to change – can we look at how you're going to keep yourself safer over the coming weeks?*

- Even if the client says that the incidents you have heard about have been exaggerated, you can say: *OK, let's plan so that you don't get in the situation again where the neighbours are calling the police because they overhear a big argument.*

- *Like a football coach going over bits of the recent matches that didn't go so well with his team, let's look back at some recent incidents to see what we can learn.*

Most people who act violently or abusively to their partners will describe this to you as 'losing control'. It is much more acceptable to think of it this way than as a deliberate or instrumental action. At the early stages of intervention, you may not be able to get your client to identify the function of violence in their life. However, you can help them to see that rather than happening without warning, there are nearly always powerful signs – like motorway warning signs – that tell us that we are building up to being abusive. If we are to do something differently what we need is alarm bells ringing as early as possible to alert us to the need to change direction. Task Sheet 3.1.1 is an exercise that you can work through with a client that will contribute to such increased awareness.

Signals work

Sore points

The first section of the task sheet asks about 'sore points'. The fact is that we rarely argue over new topics – arguments in families tend to revolve around the same broad issues or situations; some couples argue repeatedly over the division of labour, others over jealousies, others again over the time and investment each puts into the relationship. If you want to avoid being abusive, it helps to know when you're on dangerous ground, even when there's no escalation as yet. This awareness simply alerts us to proceed with caution.

Behaviour signals

As abuse escalates the signals get more obvious. The role of the worker might be to help your client notice the earlier subtler cues. The sooner they become aware that they're building up towards abuse, the easier it will be to change direction. You might use some self-disclosure of your own early signals and/or some questions like these to help your client along:

- *How do you think your partner first notices that you're annoyed/in a bad mood/getting angry?*

- *Which signals show up early in the situation and which show up later on?*

Mental state

Some people are considered 'auditory'. They will remember and notice the thoughts they have which sound like speech – their 'self-talk' – most easily. They will find it natural to come up with the phrases and comments that run through their minds as they wind themselves up. Often they'll use put-downs and swear words in their head like 'fucking idiot'. These reduce their partner to an object and an enemy – someone who deserves to be attacked. It's like propaganda against an enemy country in time of war – calling their soldiers 'military targets' and civilians 'collateral damage' or demonising the population as a way of justifying the death toll and bypassing the empathy that anyone would naturally feel if they saw the dead as real people – fathers, sons, friends, and so on.

You will find that other clients are more 'visual' and will find it easier to notice how they literally *see* the world at these times. For such people you might use the following picture, which demonstrates the gestalt switch: if you look at it one way you see an old woman; if you look at it another way you see a young woman. You can't see both at once. Sometimes we do a similar thing with our partners – there's the way we see them when we love them and the way we see them when we are annoyed and angry with them.

Divide a sheet of paper into two – if your client is artistic they can sketch in each side; if not, they can describe the two 'pictures' while you add the words: 'My partner when I feel loving or protective of them' vs 'My partner when I feel really angry with them'. Neither is the 'true' or 'false' picture, but the negative one is likely to involve turning the partner into a rather nasty caricature of themselves.

Point out how this process allows your client to see their partner as an enemy rather than the person they love and would defend to the hilt if anyone else tried to attack them. This does the same objectifying work as verbal put-downs – switching off empathy so your client can hurt their partner without hurting themselves simultaneously.

Exploring alternatives

The point of all the signals work is that if your client is aware of the escalation towards abuse, they can then take steps to prevent subsequent harmful behaviour. This is the nub of safety planning. You may do this simply by asking about what they already do to try to talk themselves down and stay safe, and from these strategies to pick the most effective single thing they can tell themselves in order to wind down.

If you've got a little more time you can go into greater depth on using 'self-talk'. Ask your client to look back at their 'mental signals' and choose two or three particularly 'risky' thoughts. Ask them to identify alternative things they can tell themselves – Information Sheet 3.1.1 may provide some examples or inspirations for this.

For more 'visual' people it might be more effective to pinpoint an image they can bring to mind that would help them to snap out of their angry and resentful mindset and wind down. Examples might be an image of their child, or a respected parent, reminding themselves of consequences, or of the look of fear on their partner's face the last time they hurt them.

Discuss how early on in the situation they have to start winding down for it to be most effective. At what point would they know this wasn't working and that it was time for a 'time out'?

You can show the information sheets at the end of the chapter to the client you are working with, taking note of the following:

- You should also give information about time outs to partners.

- This tool is designed to help the client to manage themselves, not to win arguments or to control someone else.

- 'Time out' should only be used to calm the situation, not to avoid discussion of the issue over the longer term or to avoid hearing criticism. The most common criticism made by partners of people on behaviour-change programmes is that, once they learn to take time outs, they use them to avoid responsibility by walking out when any difficult topics come up.

- In the event that your client's partner follows them when they try to take a time out, or tries to stop them leaving, they should be appropriately assertive in asking to be left alone. If this does not happen, this is not an excuse to use physical force or abuse. It is still the person's responsibility to find a non-aggressive way of handling the situation. So it is important to do some safety planning as to how they can deal with the situation non-abusively if their partner tries to prevent them from leaving.

TASK SHEET 3.1.1

Signals

Name: **Date:**

This task sheet will help to make you more aware of when you're getting into a situation where you may be abusive. The more you're aware of your signals, the more you will be able to stop yourself from being abusive.

When you notice the following signals in yourself, don't wait for them to build; do something about it!

Sore points

These are typical situations in which you've been abusive in the past – the things that really bother you. Examples might include conflicts over money, housework, children, jealousy, friends or who is right about something. You may be particularly touchy when tired, at a particular time of day,

                Kate Iwi and Chris Newman © 2015

when you're drunk or hung over, or when you've not eaten recently. Please list your typical sore points:

_____

_____

_____

_____

_____

_____

Body signals

Please list what happens for you physically at these times. What do you feel in your body – tension in your stomach/shoulders/neck/jaw, heat, changes in breathing and heart rate, etc.?

_____

_____

_____

_____

_____

_____

Behaviour signals

What do you begin to do – point a finger, close your fist, flail your arms, pace around the room, raise your voice or shout, glare, alternate between sulking and shouting, interrupt, go quiet, etc.?

_____

_____

_____

_____

_____

_____

Emotional signals

Please list your emotional signals – feeling resentful, angry, trapped, controlled, confused, persecuted, got at, challenged, guilty, embarrassed, etc:

_____

_____

_____

_____

_____

_____

Mental signals

Please list your typical thoughts at these times. These often include negative self-talk about the other person, such as: 'She's doing this deliberately to wind me up', 'She's so stupid', 'He's an idiot', 'She never gets anything right', 'She never listens to me.' Note also the things you *don't* think about, such as how the other person is feeling, trying to understand them, any of their good sides, or listening to what they say:

_____

_____

_____

_____

_____

_____

At this point you've started to be abusive and should already have started your time out. If you haven't, take a time out *now*.

INFORMATION SHEET 3.1.1

Examples of Different Kinds of Self-talk and Ways to Wind Yourself Down

Winding yourself up	Winding yourself down
Self-pity – 'Why me?'	Thinking of ways in which you're doing OK, and the choices you have
Accusing or blaming your partner	Focusing on your own behaviour and your part in what's happening. How could you do differently or better, no matter what she does?
Insulting and objectifying your partner	Humanising your partner – focusing on her feelings, trying to understand her point of view, imagining what she'd be thinking right now and so on. Reminding yourself, 'This is the woman I love', and asking yourself, 'How has she come to feel like this?'
Minimising your faults and maximising hers	Thinking of your bad points and her good ones, focusing on why you chose her and what attracted you to her
Focusing on your feelings and her behaviour	Focusing on what you did and how she felt. As a useful exercise, ask yourself, 'How could I have caused this?'
Trying to legitimise	Listing in your head all the reasons why she doesn't deserve this

Asking 'why' questions	Focusing on questions that might give you some real understanding – such as 'How would she explain her behaviour?' 'What is she feeling?'
Rehearsing an argument in your head	Rehearsing making up, apologising or sorting things out
Repeating the same points	Breaking out of repetitive thinking by using a non-collusive listener or a tool (such as a control log or writing a letter) to keep your thoughts moving forward
Imagining worst-case scenarios	Imagining best-case scenarios, or imagining making up again
Expecting to be able to exert authority	Reminding yourself of your equality – remembering she has a right to say what she's saying and to do what she's doing – and that even if you don't agree with this, you can't control her
Reminding yourself of her past wrongs	Reminding yourself what has happened before when you've wound yourself up like this – think of the consequences
Blowing it up out of proportion	Asking yourself what is really at stake here – does it really matter?
Telling yourself, 'I don't care'	Asking yourself, 'If I wasn't angry right now, what else might I be feeling? What vulnerability or hurt might I be trying to separate from?'
Focusing only on your angry emotions	Letting yourself feel hurt or vulnerable – reminding yourself that you can survive it

INFORMATION SHEET 3.1.2

Three Simple Strategies You Can Use when You Feel Yourself Escalating towards Abuse

When should I use these strategies?

Any time you recognise that these cues to your violence are present:

- you want to have an argument

- you notice your bodily signals of wanting to escalate things (e.g. heart rate, energy levels, gesturing, speaking louder, can't sit down, tension, temperature changes)

- you feel angry, jealous, righteous, trapped or any other emotions you have noticed happen when you have been abusive before

- your head is racing and you're winding yourself up – going over why you're right and she's wrong, what you can't stand about her, etc.

What can I do?

1. *Wind down*: As soon as you recognise any of these signs in yourself try to tell yourself simple things that will help to wind you down (e.g. 'It's not worth it, she's not all bad – she's also…, I can deal

with this better') or bring an image to mind that will remind you that you don't want to act that way – like your child playing, for instance.

2. *Clarify*: Stop trying to win or punish or prove your point. Start trying to get clear about what the other person is feeling and saying – begin to reflect back what you think they're saying and checking if you've got it right. Don't mock or deride their viewpoint, simply try to get clear about what they think and feel and why: 'So you're saying…because…and you want… Is that right?' This will slow down and de-escalate the argument and give you some thinking space.

3. *Take a time out?* If you're still wanting to shout at and hurt the other person then take a time out:

   ○ Leave for one hour.

   ○ Calm yourself down – go for a run, walk, find a quiet place to be for a while, whatever helps (stay safe and sober).

   ○ Wind yourself down, not up.

   ○ Return home but only if you are both ready.

Informing your partner about time outs

- It's very important to talk about time outs with your partner well ahead of when you will need to use one.

- A time out is a tool for you, not for your partner – you don't need their support to use it.

- They will only come to trust your use of time outs if you really stick to the rules.

    Kate Iwi and Chris Newman © 2015

CHAPTER 3.2

Taking Responsibility

Even if you've never attended a 12-step programme like Alcoholics Anonymous, most of us are very familiar from movies with the introduction, 'Hi, I'm…and I'm an alcoholic.' The 12-step process has a huge emphasis on acknowledgement – here are 4 of the 12 steps:

- Make a searching and fearless moral inventory of ourselves.

- Admit to a higher power, to ourselves and to another human being the exact nature of our wrongs.

- Make a list of all persons we have harmed, and become willing to make amends to them all.

- Continue to take a personal inventory, and when we are wrong promptly admit it.

What is it about the endless 'fessing up' to others that seems to be so important for making and maintaining a change? For one thing this level of acknowledgement is what motivates change – the realisation that things are not OK and, more so, that it's you who needs to change. It seems possible to amplify this effect through being witnessed and through repetition. Additionally, and importantly if you want to move your client into a perpetrator programme, it lays the groundwork for a lot of the other interventions such as CBT which require some examination of what went wrong in the past in order to put it right in the future.

Not all of our clients need to do ongoing work on acknowledgement of their abuse – you may find that the assessment stage has effectively achieved this for some people – but it's more likely than not that you'll need to revisit the process again a few weeks later.

The rope bridge to change

Share with your client the first handout of the 'rope bridge to change' (see Task Sheet 3.2.1 at the end of the chapter).

What this shows is that when you behave to those you love in ways that don't fit with how you want to be – or are expected to be – you damage your relationship and the environment you live in. You feel out of control of yourself and uneasy with how you've acted.

In your case, what have been the costs of using abuse – for you, your relationships and those around you?

Fill out the list on the left side of the bridge as costs (e.g. social services got involved; your partner's left you; your children won't talk to you; your partner is depressed).

In order to allow your life to flourish again – and those of the people you love – you need to make a journey. Imagine you've completed all this work, you've made all the changes that you want to make.

- *What do you imagine will be different?*
- *How do you imagine you might feel differently in yourself?*
- *How might people respond to the changes in you – your partner, kids, others?*

Make some notes on this on the far side of the bridge.

Now share the next rope bridge handout (see Information Sheet 3.2.1 at the end of the chapter), which shows some of the stages towards change.

Point out to your client that they've already begun the journey towards change. They have already had to step onto the bridge – to start talking to people and acknowledging what they've done and that they have a problem.

What was it like to begin talking about this?

Admitting that there's something you need to change is scary; it puts you on wobbly ground. It's horrible to feel badly about something you did. It's hard to bear criticisms or recriminations from others. Sometimes, even feeling that someone (your partner, your kids, your family, your social worker) is looking at you in a way that feels 'judgemental' can be painful.

When you come forward to face up to your actions and people don't respond quite as you want it's as if the bridge begins to rock and swing. You might begin to feel panicked, a loss of control and stability. You might fear a fall from grace – hurtling downwards towards shame and dishonour. You fear the imagined consequences of your actions (losing your family, going to prison) and these loom below you.

It's an absolutely natural reaction to begin scrambling back towards solid ground – this can be achieved by minimising and denying what you did, justifying and blaming it on others. Sometimes the very hostility that fuels our blame of others can lead us to be even more violent again. Sometimes we attack ourselves. Either way, we do more and more damage and our situation becomes more and more hostile and miserable to live in.

- *What kinds of thing/situation make you feel most defensive about what you did?*

- *How are you likely to do this – what would I see if you were feeling defensive and on your way back across this bridge in this direction?*

Refer back to the last session on denial and minimisation.

In actual fact, the only way to get away from this is to just hold on and keep moving forward over that bridge – no matter how unstable it feels, no matter that you lose all sight of the other side at times and feel like you'll never get over. You just need to hang on – and though you may not be in control, you will survive.

What can you tell yourself to keep on moving forward despite these knocks?

Soon enough you'll find you are more in control of your temper and are trying different ways to behave in your close relationships. This will remain a wobbly process for some time – just like learning to drive, it'll be clunky for a long time before it feels like it comes naturally.

As time goes on you'll begin to feel good about the way you're acting – even in difficult and conflictual situations. You'll begin to see those you hurt healing. One day you'll realise you're back on solid ground on the other side.

The Rope Bridge to Change

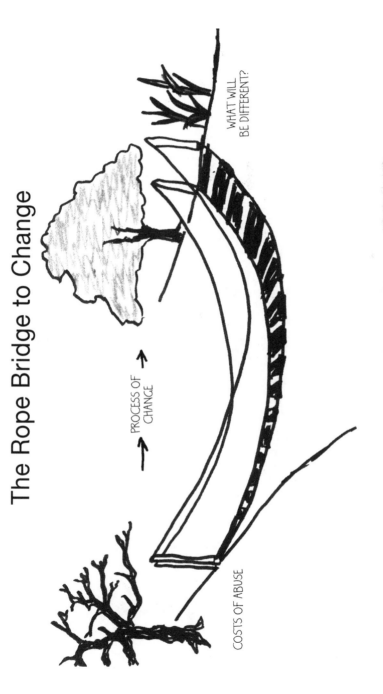

PROCESS OF CHANGE

COSTS OF ABUSE

WHAT WILL BE DIFFERENT?

Stages towards Change

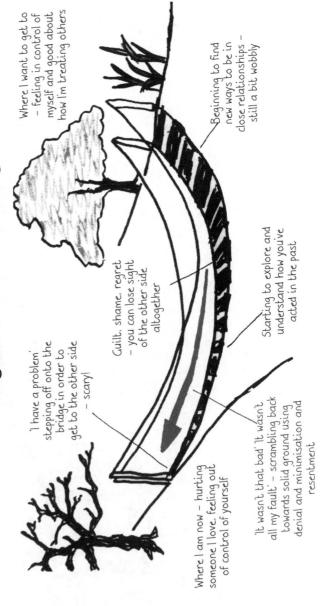

Where I want to get to – feeling in control of myself and good about how I'm treating others

Beginning to find new ways to be in close relationships – still a bit wobbly

'I have a problem' stepping off onto the bridge in order to get to the other side – scary!

Guilt, shame, regret – you can lose sight of the other side altogether

Starting to explore and understand how you've acted in the past

Where I am now – hurting someone I love, feeling out of control of yourself

'It wasn't that bad' 'It wasn't all my fault' – scrambling back towards solid ground using denial and minimisation and resentment

Extending the Definition of Abuse

Defining abuse

An essential element of working with perpetrators of domestic violence is defining what exactly we mean when we use the word 'abuse'. Once you've agreed a definition that is owned by your client themselves, then you're in a position to scrutinise a range of behaviours together and think about what seems OK and not OK.

Like all elements of this work, the best way to arrive at this is to get your client to have a go at providing their own definition, or at least to co-create one with you. The simplest way to do this is simply to ask:

What does the word 'abuse' mean to you? If you were going to explain the meaning of that word to an alien who's trying to learn to understand and recognise what counts as abuse, what would you say?

You are not at this stage seeking a list of examples, but a dictionary-like definition. In fact, the definition to be found in most dictionaries is something like this:

	Any behaviour that scares, hurts or injures someone.

You can then ask whether you can hurt or scare someone without touching them. This opens the door to extending the definition of abuse from specific acts of violence to areas such as threats, intimidation and emotional abuse.

The function of abuse

You may find that your discussions lead you quite naturally into the intent or function of abuse, but if not you will want to go on to ask:

Why do people abuse?

The answers may be wide ranging, but persist with this enquiry until your definition recognises in some sense the functional nature of abusive behaviour – the fact that it works in a number of ways:

- to win an argument
- to get the last word
- to get your own way – you can scare, pressure or wear someone down into doing something they don't want to do or stopping doing something they do want to do
- to get the power in the relationship to make the rules in future
- to punish someone and to teach them a lesson for next time
- to hurt someone and make them feel as bad as you do
- to exchange the potential for feelings of vulnerability, powerlessness and inadequacy for feelings that are much more powerful.

Many of us first learn about violence and intimidation from our parents – they shout at us, scare us and in some cases hit us, to teach us a range of lessons. Discipline based on fear and shame isn't the only way to raise children but it exists, in some form, in most families. Even if we don't come across this kind of behaviour in our families, we are very likely to come across it in school or adolescent peer groups. It is therefore hardly surprising that this model is deeply entrenched in most of us. As a result, when we don't like what someone close to us is doing or saying, we quite naturally revert to such techniques to try and stop them. These techniques are by no means limited to hitting and threatening. By the time we've made it through our teens most of us have a good handle on guilt-tripping, shouting, sarcasm and put downs, and some of us find ways to manipulate social dynamics – getting our brothers or sisters in trouble, playing one person off against another, and so on.

The following section captures a flavour of some of the most common ways of controlling intimate partners. They may not be exhaustive and certainly not *all* tactics will be used by *all* individuals. However, the examples covered should allow you to do two key things:

- *Broaden your client's understanding of what is abusive*: We often let ourselves get away with the 'lesser tactics of control' by not noticing we are using them or telling ourselves that, because they're common, they're OK. This piece of work is intended to make it more difficult for clients to deny to themselves that they are being hurtful or controlling towards those around them.

- *Obtain a wider range of behaviours to work with*: It is likely that your client will limit his or her disclosure to one or two specific incidents of physical violence, usually those that are on public record. If you restrict the focus of your work to acts of physical violence you may find yourself going over the same ground again and again, pushing for disclosure you may never achieve in your position as a social worker. Once you widen the definition of abuse, you – and those who may work with your client in future on a full perpetrator programme – will be able to work on a more realistic and complete range of behaviours and incidents and help your client work towards identifying non-abusive alternatives.

Focus one by one on each of these common ways of abusing partners – taking the time that the individual client needs (anything from 10 minutes to a full session or two) to delve into each one.

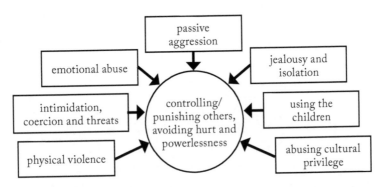

Figure 3.3.1 Common ways of controlling intimate partners

Common ways of controlling others
Physical violence

It is basic, but important, to establish with your client a shared and extended definition of violence. When you ask people whether they have ever been violent in their relationships, some may say no because they just don't include lower-level violence, like pushing or grabbing, in their definition of violence. However, the definition you establish with your client needs to take in all forms of physical contact which fit the definition of abuse given above.

Other people might be used to a broader definition of violence – one that takes in a whole gamut of non-physical abusive behaviours as well. This will get confusing and can be used as a way of minimising – for example, 'My partner was verbally violent to me so I hit her back.'

Agree with your client that when you use the word 'violence' on its own, you are referring to physical violence only – and absolutely all forms of getting physical with another person against their will.

You'll also want to be clear about what you both understand by the term 'self-defence'. With people who are a risk to their partner it's best to use a very tight definition – that is, 'the minimum level of violence a person can use to keep themselves safe if there is no other way to do so'. If a person is hit and could run away, but instead stays and hits back, that's retaliation, not self-defence. As such, the person retaliating remains 100 per cent responsible for their violence, which is a form of punishment – a way to teach their partner a lesson not to touch them again. Although children may be very preoccupied with establishing who started a fight, you'll want to focus only on whether your client could have stopped it escalating. As long as they still have a choice, they remain responsible for the option they choose.

In order to help define the scope of the concept of violence and to begin to get disclosure of as much of your client's physical abuse as you can, start by using the physical abuse inventory in Chapter 2.1. When it has been completed, you might want to ask for details of the specific incidents they are referring to. This should provide information about the range of incidents you can analyse with the help of the tools in Chapter 3.5.

Intimidation, coercion and threats

All of the following are very intimidating behaviours:

- giving 'the look'
- banging around, smashing furniture
- punching walls
- shouting
- standing over her
- pacing around
- gesticulating wildly or close to her face
- issuing orders – e.g. 'Shut up' or 'Get out'
- repeating questions without letting her answer
- getting 'in her face'
- saying you'll hurt her, yourself or the kids
- saying things like 'Make me', 'How dare you' or 'Try it'.

Point out to your client that if a person who has never been violent shows signs of anger around their partner or children, it will be unpleasant. But it is not the same if it is someone who has hit their partner or put them in physical fear in the past. After that, any signs of anger evoke the memory of the past violence and can become warning signs to their partner and children.

It may feel unfair but people who have used violence need to set themselves a higher standard of behaviour than other people. It means that even at times when they feel really unhappy, grumpy, irritated or angry they are still going to have to think about what that might look like to their partner and children, and how they can reassure them that they don't need to be afraid.

QUESTIONS TO DISCUSS WITH YOUR CLIENT

- *What effect do you think your history of using violence has on how your partner and children feel when you shout? How does that work?*

- *Mostly we don't have to make direct threats – our partners come to know that we'll withdraw affection, even safety, if they don't do what we want. In what ways might your partner feel threatened or coerced in these ways?*

- *What direct threats have you made?*

- *What's wrong with behaving like this? Why?*

- *In what practical ways can you reassure your partner and children and make them feel safe, even when you're angry or upset? (Think about your body language, the ways you move and hold your body when you are angry, the level and tone of your voice.)*

Emotional abuse

Emotional abuse is pretty much universal in intimate relationships; quite simply, almost all of us do it to one degree or another. Your client will have their own very particular way of emotionally abusing their partner. To find out more about this, some of the following are useful prompt questions:

- *How do your partner and children know to tread softly around you? What are the first signs they see?*

- *Are there particular times, situations or subjects around which they would do this? (e.g. in the morning or when you've had a drink.)*

- *What are your partner's weak spots and do you ever exploit them?*

- *What would they say if they were here?*

- *How do you see your partner when you're angry?*

- *What names do you call your partner when you're angry?*

- *What's wrong with behaving like this? Why?*

Information Sheet 3.3.1 at the end of the chapter is a long list of emotionally abusive tactics; go through this with your client and find out what they recognise themselves as using.

Passive aggression

There are a number of ways of showing our anger and achieving similar outcomes in terms of controlling others without being outwardly aggressive at all. These sorts of behaviours are what we call passive aggressive. Many of us have a range of these tactics, some of which can be quite subtle. There's a danger that those of us who are more self-aware around being abusive can get increasingly covert about the way we do it – and that such undercover abuse can be used as a replacement for overt aggression once the latter is under the microscope of children's services. As with all the tactics discussed, some people don't have a big range in this area. In such cases, simply skip to the sections you think are relevant.

Passive aggression is easiest to define by example – it includes:

- sulking
- giving in without meaning it
- sighing
- muttering
- sarcasm
- mimicry
- ignoring
- guilt-tripping
- fake crying
- not owning up to feelings
- withdrawing cooperation
- giving clipped, brief answers
- making faces/rolling eyes
- saying things like, 'I'm not angry, I'm just disappointed in you.'

You can make admitting to the ways we do this a relatively light piece of work – ideally bringing in the odd 'safe enough' example of your own. You may find that for your client a lot of the earliest signs of a build up towards violence are of this nature, so it is a useful discussion to have to increase awareness of his own 'signals'. On the other hand, some couples can maintain sulking for days or even years. There's no doubt, though, that this kind of silent resentment will eat away at them, their partner and their children.

Jealousy and isolation

Jealousy is a pervasive problem in some people's lives. You are likely to come across some couples for whom it has been the main issue they have argued over. The fear of abandonment and betrayal for many people dates back to earliest childhood and is intimately bound up with their attachment style. For some, jealousy may be linked with previous experiences in adult relationships. For others, it may hardly figure at all in the family dynamic.

So, depending on your client, jealousy is an issue you may just touch on, or you may need to linger there briefly, or you may want to spend a few sessions focusing solely on this subject.

Being obsessively or morbidly jealous is a very strong indicator for risk of future violence, particularly at times when the client feels the relationship is under threat. However, it is perhaps in your favour that the repetitive thinking patterns and powerful feelings associated with jealousy are intensely distressing for the person who feels this way, which can give rise to a real motivation to change.

First you'll want to explore how much of a problem it is for this person. Ask them to think of one or more people with whom they would rather their partner did not have contact. Almost everyone can think of someone.

Now ask how they show this:

- *How would your partner know that you were jealous?*
- *What kinds of things do you do when you are jealous?*

Present and elicit some examples of the kinds of things some people do when jealous (being careful not to give away inventive ideas such as hi-tech surveillance). You could say something like:

> *Some people make it uncomfortable for their partner to see that person, by all sorts of means, from behaving sulkily to forbidding it. Others check up on their partner, texting or calling a lot or looking at their phone messages. Some again interrogate their partners when they feel jealous. Have you ever done that kind of thing?*

Make a list of a range of such behaviours, from subtle to directly coercive.

Ask why people who are jealous try to isolate their partners in these ways. What do they fear? Usually, the ultimate fear is abandonment. With sexual jealousy this usually amounts to the fear that the partner will meet someone else. When the isolating behaviour seems to be more focused on friends or family members, there is often an underlying fear that these particular people will influence the partner against your client or expose them to other opportunities to leave the relationship. *Ensure that your client can see that jealous behaviour is ultimately aimed at stopping the partner leaving and/or alleviating unbearable feelings of insecurity.*

As with violence, there may be a short-term pay off to jealous behaviour – for example, the partner may well be put off from going out with someone who is considered a 'threat'. Acknowledge this point but draw your client's attention to the longer-term effects of jealous behaviour.

Once you actually look at the impacts of the behaviour – on the jealous party, on his partner and on their relationship – it's easy to grasp that this behaviour is self-defeating in the longer term.

Most people who have intense feelings of insecurity can relate these back to early childhood experiences such as parental abandonments (which may have been temporary and partial or permanent and total) or lack of parental availability (due to parental depression, trauma or illness, or simply sharing with siblings). People don't feel more secure by acting in a jealous and controlling way, precisely because the reasons we feel jealous relate to difficulty living with our own insecurities, and to low self-esteem. Trying in any way to control a partner's behaviour doesn't affect that, and in fact can make the feelings worse.

Here are some prompt questions, which can help you explore this with your client:

So we have established that when you act in a jealous way, you are seeking to stop your partner leaving you and/or to get rid of these horrible feelings of insecurity that eat away at you.

- *When you've questioned your partner, do you feel less jealous or more secure?*
- *Do you feel better if your partner says your fears are true?*
- *If your partner reassures you that your fears are unfounded, do you believe him/her or do you just think, 'S/he's saying that to reassure me'?*
- *How does your jealous behaviour make your partner feel?*
- *How will this affect the relationship?*
- *How will this affect your partner's behaviour?*
- *Will your partner be more likely to stay in the long run?*

As you talk, listen out for hints or outright statements of the belief system that support the jealousy – for example:

▪ If s/he hangs around with people who don't like me s/he will take on their views and will leave me.
▪ If she is friendly with another man that is flirting.
▪ If s/he is allowed to flirt with other people s/he will leave me.
▪ All other men are predatory and trying to get her to sleep with them.
▪ If s/he wants to flirt with other people s/he wants to sleep with them.
▪ If s/he flirts with or is attracted to others there will be 'less of her/him' available to me.
▪ If s/he flirts with others then I will be a laughing stock.
▪ Most people have affairs given half a chance.
▪ Relationships cannot survive affairs.
▪ If s/he has sex with someone else this is the worst thing in the world.
▪ If s/he 'betrays' me I will not survive.
▪ If s/he 'betrays' me I will be terribly humiliated.
▪ The only way I would feel better again would be to get revenge.

The roots of these kinds of beliefs in your client's personal and cultural history can be examined – many of them are swallowed wholesale without being thought through. Most of all, your client needs to be encouraged to think outside the box. Ask your client to imagine and talk about exceptions to these 'rules' – even to imagine a world where these codes weren't right at all.

> *Some people live this way now. Some people don't mind if their partners flirt with other people – even feel proud that people are attracted to their partner – without feeling threatened in any way by that. How do you think they manage that?*

> *Do you know anyone who is in a relationship that survived an affair?*

> *Have you ever enjoyed a mild flirtation but wouldn't want to sleep with that person?*

No matter how much you gently chip away at the belief systems underlying jealousy, it's likely the feelings will remain. Much of the family dynamic in which the insecurity will first have taken root will be early, pre-verbal and inaccessible to short 'talking cures'.

> *You may be left with incredibly difficult and uncomfortable feelings and obsessive thoughts. However, the reality is that the more you fuel your obsessional jealous feelings by checking up on and questioning your partner, the longer those feelings will continue.*

What you can help your client to do is to take a step away and learn to distance themselves from the jealous feelings.

You might get them to draw something – maybe just a scribble on a piece of paper – that can represent the jealousy. Then just put it on a chair far away from them and begin to talk about it – ask what energy or vibe it has, whether it has a tone of voice, what it tells your client about their partner or the world and how they know when it's around.

Ask them how they have ever held it at bay or begun to feel better in the past. Whatever they did (e.g. distraction, counter-thoughts) they can develop into a more conscious strategy. They can begin simply to notice jealousy whenever it appears and to distance themselves from it in this way.

Given that we've seen the link between jealousy and self-esteem, you might ask your client what they can do to make them feel good about themselves when they get jealous. This is the only real way to interrupt the vicious circle of jealous behaviour leading to even more jealous feelings.

Example answers:

- Building up emotional muscle (the ability to tolerate feelings of neediness and dependency)
- Building up social networks that won't support your jealousy. Which friends do you have who wouldn't collude?
- Positive self-talk, especially accepting that this is the way you feel, and that she's not making you feel like that – she's not making you jealous
- Accepting that it won't work in terms of getting what you want, if that is to feel more secure
- Recognising that you're jealous and that your beliefs about what is going on are likely to be severely warped by this, and using that energy on something constructive to feel proud of. For example, you can go to the gym, take the children out, make something or learn something
- Doing something you've always wanted to do
- Letting go the beliefs that we have any rights over who our partners see or what they do. Your partner is in a relationship with you because she chooses to be. If she stops choosing to be in it, there is nothing ultimately that you can do about it. You will survive it.

Using the children

It's actually difficult not to involve children in adult arguments even if you try, and it is harder still if you think the other parent is using the children to get at you. The image of two parents tearing their child in two whilst telling themselves they are acting 'out of love' fits a lot of our cases.

Figure 3.3.2 Pulling the kids apart

Also, once social services have become involved, the children know only too well that they should be careful what they say. Often they are rent with anxiety that they might say 'the wrong thing' whilst not really knowing what that is.

Where there's a pattern of coercive control in the relationship, the children are bound to be used by the abusive parent in some way or another. However, this is one of the areas where parents find it hardest to face up to what they've been doing.

Look together with your client at each item on Information Sheet 3.3.2 at the end of the chapter and make a list of the potential effects on children if parents behave in these ways.

It is important not to allow either parent to get into a tit-for-tat on this issue. They must put the children's needs first even if the other parent doesn't. Their only concern should be that they behave in the best possible manner for their children's wellbeing and security. Getting caught up in monitoring each other's parenting or avenging their hurt feelings will always get in the way of this. As the social worker it's important that you take on the role of promoting the children's best interests with both parents and helping them to see that the more they pull, the more they tear their children apart. Especially for the perpetrator, who must learn to let go of controlling their ex-partner, it is vital that they begin to focus exclusively on their own parenting.

Note: If your client is avoiding talking about their own behaviour by focusing on the ways in which they think their (ex-)partner is using the children against them, hold in mind some of the points from the section above on minimisation and blame.

> *Let's assume for the moment that your partner isn't going to change, and let's focus on how you've responded when you don't like what they are doing.*
>
> *I know that you want the best for your children. In what ways can you protect them from getting involved in the conflict? Can you let go of some of the anger and resentment for their sake? If you did that and held in mind just what is best for the children, how would you handle this situation?*

Information Sheet 3.3.3 at the end of the chapter is about child contact for dads who've been abusive to the mum. There is without doubt work that often needs doing with mothers too about how they are with the children. You'll find plenty more on that in our book *Picking up the Pieces After Domestic Violence*.[1]

Abusing cultural privilege

This tactic is explored in detail in Chapter 3.4.

---

1   Jessica Kingsley Publishers, 2011.

INFORMATION SHEET 3.3.1
Emotional Abuse

Emotional abuse is about:

- putting her down
- making her feel bad about herself
- calling her names
- making her think she's crazy
- playing mind games
- humiliating her
- making her feel guilty.

Emotional abuse includes:

- *swearing and general, often sexual, put-downs*: 'fucking cow', 'bitch', 'piece of shit', 'slut', 'tart', 'flirt', 'whore', 'useless'

- *making her feel stupid, or writing off her viewpoint*: 'You're stupid/ignorant', 'You don't understand'

- *making her feel crazy, or writing off her viewpoint on the basis that she's irrational*: 'You're hysterical', 'You're mad', 'You've got a problem', 'You've got PMT'

- *getting calm just when she gets angry and then mocking her*: 'Look at the state of you'

- *writing off her viewpoint by exaggerating it and making it seem ridiculous or by using sarcasm*: 'So you want me to keep a logbook of every single penny

I spend?', 'Shall I go around with a pair of blinkers on so I can't even see other women?'

- *deflecting a problem from you to her by making out she's irrationally obsessed by it*: 'You're always nagging about that', 'You're obsessive about tidiness', 'You're paranoid'

- *lying to her and then making out she's got a problem with trust*: 'You're always imagining I'm out with other women', 'You're always questioning me about my drinking'

- *putting her down or writing off her viewpoint on the basis of her class, race, culture, religion or gender*: 'That's just middle-class bullshit', 'That's typical of a woman (or Italian, Christian, etc.)', 'You'll never understand because you're not a proper Muslim (or European or …)'

- *getting at her weak spots and making her feel unattractive or bad about herself*: 'You're fat (or ugly, useless, etc.)', 'You can't hold a job down', 'You're just like your mother', 'You embarrass yourself in front of your friends', 'Nobody else would have you'

- *making her feel incompetent, comparing her with past partners*: 'You're not fit to be a mother', 'You're frigid', 'You drive like an idiot', 'You can't cook', 'You're clumsy', 'My wife never minded me doing that – how come you go on about it all the time?'

- *answering a criticism with a counter-criticism, or an accusation with a counter-accusation*: 'Yeah, well, it pisses me off when you …too', 'You think you're such a bloody angel – what about the time when you …'

- *bringing in other people's opinions as if to prove your point*: 'Billy thinks you were out of order too', 'My mum's always said you were a bad mother'

- *dodging her criticisms and making her feel crazy by flat-out denying things or arguing over tiny details*: 'I did not say you were flirting – I just said it was bloody odd behaviour', 'I didn't kick you', 'I am not shouting', 'I am not angry', 'It was only seven times, actually – not ten'

- *putting her down by devaluing her work, her interests or her friends*: 'It's just a poxy low-paid little job', 'You're just a housewife', 'Your mates are just a bunch of brainless bimbos'

- *mocking her by agreeing without meaning it at all, or by making insincere apologies or promises*: 'Yeah, yeah, yeah, sure I was wrong', 'Whatever!', 'Look, I'm sorry. Now is that enough?'

- *overlooking her anger and her underlying needs by focusing on the smallness of her complaints*: 'It's no big deal', 'You're making a mountain out of a molehill'

- *putting her down in front of others by using any of these tactics*: ordering her to do things, displaying your dominance publicly, touching her sexually in public when she isn't receptive, bringing up stories and jokes about her that you know she wouldn't want aired publicly

- *refusing to consider changing your behaviour*: 'I'm just made like that – take it or leave it', 'It's the way I am.'

The cumulative outcome of such tactics can be that:

- she feels so guilty, bad about herself, insecure or stupid (and/or ugly, crazy, unheard) that she becomes withdrawn, resentful, angry and depressed

- you don't have to look at your behaviour, so you don't have to change
- the argument is diverted elsewhere and the problem never gets solved
- you both feel that she's the one with the problem, the one who needs help and has to change
- she feels more insecure about herself and more dependent on you, so she finds it harder to leave
- she stays only because she hasn't got the confidence in herself to leave
- she remains unhappy and you remain unhappy
- the relationship moves further away from intimacy, honesty and respect.

TASK SHEET 3.3.2

Ways in Which Children Get Used in Disputes

Ways in which children get used in disputes between parents	
Encouraging the children to take sides	
Putting the other parent down to the children	
Making the other parent feel guilty about the children	
Using child contact to harass your ex-partner	
Using contact/custody cases to continue your argument	
Using children to relay messages	
Using children to check up on your (ex-)partner	
Threatening to take the children away	
Making your partner 'control' the children in order to protect them from punishment from you	
Using the children as confidantes	

INFORMATION SHEET 3.3.2

Ways in Which Children Get Used in Disputes

Ways in which children get used in disputes between parents	Effects of this behaviour on the child
Encouraging the children to take sides	It confuses them – 'splits them down the middle'
Putting the other parent down to the children	They lose respect for the parent who's being got at, which hurts them because they want to love and admire their parents Or they feel upset and defensive on behalf of the parent being put down Or they'll feel angry with the parent who's running down the other
Making the other parent feel guilty about the children	Damages their parenting (and so hurts the children)
Using child contact to harass your ex-partner	Hurts the children because they either see the arguments or sense them and they feel like they're right in the middle
Using contact/custody cases to continue your argument	Both parents are stressed all the time – which worries and confuses the children

Using children to relay messages	The children might get blamed They might have to deal with parents' angry or upset reactions, but more likely they might have to become 'little diplomats' anxiously trying to manage their parents' conflicts
Using children to check up on your (ex-)partner	They feel bad to one parent if they do tell and bad to the other if they don't They might feel really guilty and overly responsible for both parents
Threatening to take the children away	Children feel terrified that they are going to lose their mum or dad
Making your partner 'control' the children in order to protect them from punishment from you	The children live in fear of both parents
Using the children as confidantes	Children are overburdened They become very anxious and confused because they are not equipped to handle adult issues and emotions

INFORMATION SHEET 3.3.3

Tips for Separated Fathers

If you are a father who has been abusive in a relationship with the mother of your children and you are now separated it can be very difficult knowing how best to deal with the children and your ex-partner. You may need to adapt some of the following guidelines to fit your situation, as every situation is different. However, there is one main thing to remember. It doesn't matter what the circumstances were, or whose fault you think it was, or if you think you have changed, or if it wasn't in front of the children or if you think they didn't get your side of the story: children don't like people hurting either of their parents. You hurting or abusing their mum almost certainly affected them and probably still does. They may be scared, upset or angry at you.

Understand that your children are likely to be very confused about their feelings for both you and their mum. It is possible to feel lots of different emotions at the same time and children's feelings can also change quite quickly over time. Pre-teen children are usually concrete thinkers who prefer to see the world as black and white – good guys and bad guys – rather than in shades of grey. Thus, loving a father who has been violent can be bewildering for them.

Boundaries

Minimise situations where children see you and your ex-partner together. With high conflict or continuing threats, no contact at all between parents is the best thing for the children.

Don't think you have to be friends with your ex-partner. Aim for a working relationship – 'cooperative colleagues' is the ideal. Letting go of a partner when you may not be ready or under circumstances that feel unfair is one of the hardest things in the world to do. If you try to avoid all unnecessary contact, the resentment/grief stages will pass more easily for both of you.

Be clear about your boundaries with your ex. Even casual or trivial displays of affection between ex-partners can be confusing for children, delaying them coming to terms with the separation.

Don't let your kids see you being abusive to anyone. That even includes other drivers on the roads. You may scare them and it will make it harder for them to rebuild their trust in you. 'Not in front of the children' applies even more now to arguments with your ex. Be insistent that you don't argue or have serious discussions when the children are around. This is not the time to discuss arrangements or issues (do this by phone or e-mail). Once there has been high conflict in a family, raised voices can have a different meaning for children for years to come. You can't win in this situation as many children are hypersensitive to tone of voice, body language and facial expressions, and any negativity between you will be stressful to them.

Stop shouting at your children, threatening them, putting them down or hitting them. But continue to discipline them by rewarding good behaviour and explaining why bad behaviour is wrong – setting firm but gentle consequences. They may act like you've gone soft at first but they will gradually learn to respect your new way of doing things. Children who have been through parental separation and conflict need gentle treatment for a prolonged period to help them through.

Avoid criticism of the other parent as far as possible. Not only is this upsetting and stressful for children but criticism can backfire as children often defend, openly or mentally, a parent who is attacked. If the children tell you that your ex-partner is criticising you, don't believe you can even the score by criticising her. Just state that this is their mother's opinion and you don't agree – people often see the same situation differently. Try not to show your anger. It may be helpful to find someone neutral, such as a counsellor, for the children to talk to about this. Don't expect the children to be able to stand up to their mother – even if they know she is exaggerating or they say they hate her criticising you, they probably won't be able to say anything to her.

Avoid talking to other people about your ex-partner when the kids are around, as even if you can resist being critical, your friends and family will often say things that are hurtful to the children.

Accountability

Try to model being accountable for your behaviour irrespective of whether you think their mother is doing so too. Think of this as a way of teaching the children how to face up to their own mistakes rather than as anything to do with arguing for their loyalties (although they are very likely to appreciate your frank honesty). Don't criticise their mum but do own up to your own faults.

Don't make excuses for any of your abusive or seriously irresponsible behaviour – if you do make excuses they may grow up thinking that abuse is acceptable or normal, greatly increasing the chances that they will repeat or accept such behaviour in the future.

You might say something like this but in your own words:

> I have done some things that are not right, such as hitting Mummy or scaring you. I am really sorry for doing these things and for how much it has upset you. A lot of families have problems like this even though they might not tell people about it. I still love you. It isn't even a bit your fault – you're too young/small to be able to control us or to stop us arguing. There is no excuse for me hitting Mummy or you. Violence is wrong, no matter how angry you get. No matter what you do, you don't deserve to be hit.

Loyalty

Children often struggle very hard to be loyal to their parents. Loyalty conflicts can be intense (usually worst around ages 12 to 14), with children sometimes not only turning against new partners but against brothers and sisters and even against their mother (often temporarily) as they try to resolve their loyalty conflicts. Some children say they feel as if they are pawns in their parents' games or that they are being torn in two. It can be an extremely hard balancing act – trying to protect your children without taking part in a tug of war.

Loyalty conflicts may make it very hard for them to open up to you about their mother or about their feelings. Don't push them to tell you everything. Don't interrogate them about what happens with their mother or they will learn to lie or clam up. They also may find it hard to talk to you about the situation because they are protective of you and don't want to see you upset.

Don't assume that your ex has 'poisoned the children against you'. They are most likely angry with you for their own reasons. They may also be angry with you because their mum is upset and they feel loyal to her. That doesn't mean she's done this on purpose. Children usually see right away when one parent is trying to turn them against the other and more often than not they end up very angry with the manipulative parent.

Mum's new partner

Don't rush to conclusions about their mother's new partner. Often the new person around can be intensely hated because of the loyalty issues described above, or can represent the new, fun person around who's really working to win them over – in short, your children could really like or hate the new man around their mother without it showing much about what he's actually like. They may tell you they like him just to get at you if they feel confused or angry with you. Or they may say they hate him just to please you.

Don't think for a minute that because their mother finds a new partner, he will replace you. Even if the children really like him (for which you should be glad, even if it pains you), the bond they have with him will be nothing like that which they have with you. Sometimes new people can be a lot of fun, without them really mattering.

Contact

You want to see your child. It's natural and normal for you to feel that way. For your child and your ex, it might not be so straightforward. You're the adult and the parent, so no matter what's happened, no matter what the reasons are for the lack of contact and no matter who or what you think is to blame for this, you have to be able to put all this aside and do what's best for your child.

The good news is that most women, even after violence, *do* want their children to know their dad and for him to be involved regularly, provided it is *safe* for all of them, including her. You might have to do some work to convince everyone that it is safe and they might take a long time to believe you. You will have to be patient – just because you think you have changed, you can't expect everyone else to feel the same way.

Beware of making unrealistic demands and instead let trust build. If you use contact reliably and not ever in bargaining other things (e.g. finances) or being abusive, then your ex is more likely to come to recognise the benefits of it to herself and the children.

No matter how long it takes before your child is ready for contact, you will still have to make sure that this is OK for their mum. If she is still frightened of you it will be vital to make sure that the contact doesn't make this worse, otherwise it will also affect your children. For example, you may have to arrange to pick the children up from a child contact centre, or start off by having only indirect contact for a while or supervised contact at a child contact centre.

Don't overcommit – regularity is more important for children than frequency. It is far better that children see their father predictably once a month than fortnightly but with lots of cancellations. If every day is a potential contact day then every day can be a disappointment or rejection to them.

Be very reliable with whatever contact you have. If you aren't, it confuses children and creates opportunities for more trauma and stress. At times of great upset and change, creating new, reliable routines is vital.

Think of yourself as having responsibilities to your children rather than rights to them. Ask yourself how well you are fulfilling your responsibilities in the circumstances, rather than whether you're getting what you want from this.

Make the most of the contact you have – write letters, take pictures and make albums of your time together, and talk a lot to your children about their lives and interests as well as your own and your family's. Do activities that allow for interaction – from playing to helping with homework or cooking together, to special memorable trips out (though these should not dominate your time with the children).

You can't make it up to your children by spoiling them – and they will see through it and lose respect for you.

Finally

Dealing with all this is like walking through an emotional minefield! Don't feel that you are a failure if you need to ask for help for yourself or for your children. A few children may need a lot of help, but some benefit from just a few counselling sessions with an independent adult or time with a loving grandparent.

Looking after yourself is very important for your children's wellbeing. Getting your own life back on track may be the best way to help the children.

If the other parent is being irresponsible you have to be more responsible with regard to the kids. Don't ever let your adherence to any of these guidelines depend on how well the children's mother is doing. Don't sink to their level or play tit for tat with your children's wellbeing.

CHAPTER 3.4

Abusing Cultural Privilege

Exploiting power relationships that already exist is not a *necessary* feature of domestic abuse, but it's *often* involved, fuelling one party's sense of entitlement over the other and/or limiting the options of the victim to stand their ground or leave.

To begin with, it will help to discuss the main axes of power that exist in the wider society. From there you can go on to explore how your client's particular relationship intersects with each of these.

Show your client the list of groups in Task Sheet 3.4.1 and ask them to assign numbers to them according to the relative power of the groups. 1 indicates that the group generally has greater power, 2 indicates less power, but more power than 3, and so on. For example, if your client feels men generally have greater power than women, in the first line he would score 'men' as 1 and 'women' as 2.

Some of the power relationships might be hard to figure out and might need some real discussion. It might help to think about the difference between having more and less societally sanctioned power.

Attributes of more powerful groups tend to be: strength, autonomy, access to resources, being able to demand or order, making the decisions, making the rules, or being able to punish. *Attributes of less powerful groups* are more along the lines of: being given choices, using manipulation, asking for, having to seduce or guilt trip, or defiance and resistance, which often leads to punishment.

For some of the groups on the list there are clearly correct answers, but for many it's a matter of opinion, and it is interesting to explore in which contexts one group may become more powerful.

Point out how each individual can sometimes be in a more powerful group and sometimes in a less powerful group. Ask your client to tell you about some times they've found themselves in the less powerful group.

Figure 3.4.1 Differential power of groups

How did they feel they were treated by the more powerful group, especially in negative ways?

Figure 3.4.2 Treatment of less powerful groups

Divide a sheet of paper into two columns. Write the verbs your client uses into one of the columns. Examples might include: disrespected, ignored, devalued, silenced, excluded, invisible, abused, exploited, mistreated, talked down to, dismissed and patronised.

Now enquire as to how they would have wanted to be treated by the more powerful group. Write those verbs in the second column. Examples might include: acknowledged, respected, included, consulted, considered and validated.

Write in titles for these two columns: 'Abusing power' and 'Behaving well with power'.

Return to Task Sheet 3.4.1. and ask your client to mark all those axes on which he has more power than his partner. Explain that you are going to look more closely at the areas they have identified, to think about how they have used that power. You can then use the resources in the rest of this chapter to identify and discuss specific examples.

The rest of this chapter is designed so that you can select what is relevant to your client – the areas where your client does have more power than their partner.

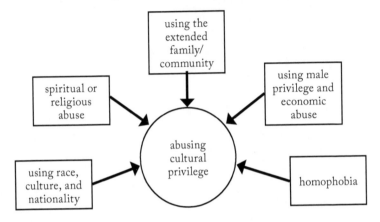

Figure 3.4.3 Ways we can abuse cultural privilege

Common ways of abusing cultural privilege

Using race, culture and nationality

Race, culture and nationality are three different, but often convergent, axes along which power differentials exist in couple relationships. The more extreme power differentials appear in cases where one person comes from overseas, leaving their own family and culture for a relationship or marriage with a partner in a foreign land. The person can so easily find themselves isolated and disempowered in terms of their ability to access support – due both to gaps in their knowledge of the system and also to linguistic barriers.

There are a number of ways that the abuser may exacerbate and exploit this power differential. The list below can be used as an abuse inventory with your client, a way to open discussion of different kinds of abuse and to check off what they have used in their own relationship:

- discouraging her from linking up with support systems beyond your own family
- putting her down for her 'uneducated' or 'unsophisticated' ways
- discouraging her from learning English
- threatening that she can't stay here if she doesn't do what you want
- keeping her dependent, for example by not allowing her to receive child benefits directly
- saying that she and her family are not good enough for you and yours
- keeping her from knowing her rights, and the practical and legal support that she's entitled to
- telling her that it's wrong to break up the family
- enlisting other members of the community or a representative of your religion to pressure her to stay or behave as you want her to
- refusing to treat her as an equal
- not taking her viewpoints into account
- treating her like a slave – getting her to stay at home and do all the housework
- not sharing opportunities equally with her for social life or work life
- telling her that she should maintain her traditional responsibilities while you do not uphold all of yours
- insisting that she choose the same level of tradition or religious practice in her life as you do.

Where your client is using culture and immigration against his partner, ask him to imagine himself in her position – if he were isolated within her family and country, for example.

How would he like to be treated? Return to the verbs on the 'Behaving well with power' list and ask him to think about what they'd look like in practice in his relationship.

You might also find out if there are people within his own family and culture who would disapprove of his abusive behaviour by asking if he's told everyone around him (family, religious community, etc.) about it. If not, why not?

Spiritual or religious abuse

For some of us, religion is a marginal or non-existent part of modern life. For others it remains an absolutely core part of their life, and spiritual or religious considerations come into everything they do. It's unsurprising then that there are a range of ways that religious and spiritual beliefs can be exploited, such as:

- telling her that religion requires her to forgive, endure or submit to her lot
- telling her that religion abhors separating the family and that she will be to blame if she leaves for her safety
- threatening to use curses or other magic on her
- claiming that her anger is a sign of possession or sinfulness.

Using the extended family/community

Some of us, especially in the West, have little involvement with extended family nowadays, but we all have a social circle of some sort. Some of us are still deeply embedded in traditional social structures and these continue to provide us with huge amounts of support, practical help and guidance as well as our sense of community and identity.

Find out about others who are involved in this couple's relationship. Who do they both go to for support and guidance? Try to get a sense of the perspectives of those around the couple. Which of them are forces for safety and would support her getting safe, even if it meant leaving the relationship? Which of them are forces for holding them together, no matter what? Who is seen to be on whose 'side'?

In some cases an abuser can use these social and familial relationships around the couple to coerce, manipulate and abuse his partner further – for example by:

- telling her that she will ruin the family's honour or reputation if she leaves for her safety
- not protecting her from extended family who directly abuse her physically or emotionally
- letting extended family instigate or encourage him to use abuse
- using family members to check up on, isolate and police the victim
- using extended family to mediate and ultimately to exert pressure on her to stay or go back
- saying she will have to return her dowry or otherwise pay back the extended family if she leaves for her safety
- threatening to 'out' him or her in a same sex relationship.

Using male privilege and economic abuse

Male privilege may not be what it used to be – in the 20 years that the writers of this book have been in the field, we've seen a definite decrease in violence over 'getting the food on the table on time'. But while social norms may have shifted for many of us, male entitlement is still very much alive and kicking, and the power relationship between men and women is still the power differential that governs the way a lot of DV operates. You'll need to investigate how far this is the case in your client's relationship. Who does what roles? Who makes what decisions? Who earns more money? How is the money divided and spent and how is this decided? Who gets to spend more time in the public realm (at work or out socially)? Whose libido defines the pace of the sexual relationship? Is the man's greater physical power used to win arguments?

While gender equality doesn't mean being the same, it does mean having the same level of choice as the other. Find out how far your client exploits traditional male entitlement – for example by:

- preventing her working
- deciding who has what roles
- making her ask and be grateful for money
- treating her like a servant
- making all the big decisions
- doing the lion's share of the socialising
- denying her knowledge about the family income
- setting the pace and content of the sexual relationship
- using gendered put-downs and double standards ('You slut!', 'Stupid woman', etc.)
- always being the one in the driving seat or with the remote control
- acting like his role is more important than hers.

Again, return to the verbs on the 'Behaving well with power' list and discuss what they would look like in practice in his relationship.

Homophobia

Note that in same sex relationships, despite both partners apparently being oppressed within wider society, one partner may harness homophobia – both internalised and in wider society – to oppress and control the other. Again, check through the tactics below with your client and tease out some detail of any of the tactics they've used:

- threatening to 'out' your partner
- using homophobic abuse against your partner
- questioning if they're a 'real' lesbian, gay, man or woman
- defining how a same sex relationship should be and defining your partner's role
- justifying behaviours that hurt your partner as being 'normal' in same sex relationships (e.g. sex with other people).

TASK SHEET 3.4.1

The Relative Power of Groups

- men ☐; women ☐

- elders ☐; adults ☐; children ☐

- White people ☐; Black African people ☐;
  Asian people ☐

- Americans ☐; Africans ☐; English ☐;
  Eastern Europeans ☐; Bangladeshis ☐
  [add as needed to cover your client and his partner]

- Muslim ☐; Jew ☐; Christian ☐

- weaker ☐; stronger ☐

- surrounded by family ☐; isolated from family ☐

- asylum seeker on own application ☐; asylum seeker
  on partner's application ☐; illegal immigrant ☐;
  citizen ☐; person with indefinite leave to remain ☐

- able bodied ☐; alternatively abled ☐

- has less knowledge of the culture ☐; has more knowledge of the culture ☐

- in bad health ☐; in good health ☐

- director ☐; unemployed ☐; employee ☐; manager ☐

- less educated ☐; more educated ☐

- richer ☐; poorer ☐

- upper class ☐; working class ☐; middle class ☐

- wage earner ☐; housewife ☐

- lots of friends ☐; few friends ☐

- in a same sex relationship but not 'out' ☐; in a heterosexual relationship ☐; in a same sex relationship and 'out' ☐

- police officer ☐; civilian ☐; person serving in the army ☐

- English as second language ☐; English as mother tongue ☐; non-English speaking ☐.

CHAPTER 3.5

Analysing Incidents of Abuse

This part of the work uses a basic storyboard format to unpack an incident of abuse, and in particular to consider how an individual's self-talk influences their feelings and, ultimately, their behaviour.

You can explain that what you are going to do is similar to what a football coach does after a match that hasn't gone well: they get the team in and go back over a video of the match, replaying it and looking in detail at what went wrong and what they could have done differently.

Storyboards

Below is an example storyboard showing how you might work with each stage. The scenes in the example storyboard show:

- how the incident started
- what was happening just before the violence or abuse
- what happened during the violence or abuse
- the aftermath of the violence or abuse
- how the situation could have been handled differently.

You will use the example scenes as prompts to help your client draw their own storyboard. Then each scene will be looked at in detail, to help you and your client understand their actions, thoughts and feelings better and think together about ways to act differently.

Note: Whilst we have set out an incident of violence here, you can use this technique to unpack any incident of physical or verbal aggression or emotional abuse.

We begin with the example storyboards, which relate to a man called Carl, his partner Pat and their child Ali (aged 2). When doing this kind of work we have found it useful to start out by working on a third party example rather than the client's own situation. This way the client can start to explore the thoughts and feelings that are associated with abusive behaviour without their own emotions getting in the way. Once you have unpicked an imaginary example, it is easier to move on to the client's own situation.

In the example (see below) Carl has drawn a series of scenes relating to a time he was abusive to Pat, and has written a brief description of what was going on at each stage.

After you have shown Carl's scenes, your client should be ready to sketch and describe their own (they can add in extra scenes if they think that is helpful). If they are unwilling or unable to attempt this, then do it for them under their direction – drawing skill is not relevant to this exercise *at all*. It is good to do this on a large piece of paper so there is lots of room for ideas.

Hints and tips: When you take a description of each stage of the incident, try to get your client to leave out value judgements such as 'She was flirting' or 'She was disrespecting me' and see if they can instead describe the behaviours they call 'flirting' or 'disrespecting'.

For instance:

> 'She was flirting with all the men at the party.' → 'She was talking and laughing with some of the men at the party.'
>
> 'Her daughter Kelly was disrespecting me.' → 'Kelly looked at me blankly, then walked out of the room.'

This ensures you're not tacitly colluding with these value judgements, and leaves the possibility open that your client might also come to interpret events in a different way.

You can now set about doing different pieces of work with each picture in the storyboard. See below for a summary of how you would work with each stage.

Carl's storyboard and how to work on each stage with your client

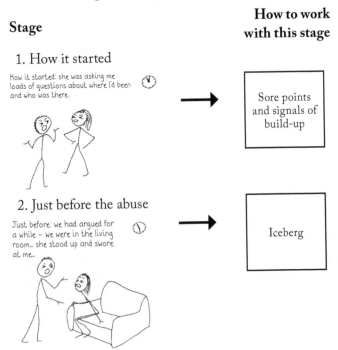

Stage	How to work with this stage
1. How it started How it started: she was asking me loads of questions about where I'd been and who was there.	Sore points and signals of build-up
2. Just before the abuse Just before: we had argued for a while – we were in the living room... she stood up and swore at me...	Iceberg

3. During the abuse

During: I punched her back onto the sofa and went on hitting her. I got her one time on the face and then 3 or 4 times on the back and shoulder.

> What did he do/say? How did she feel? Let's imagine the kids heard this – how would they have felt?

4. The aftermath

The aftermath: Someone must have called the police – they banged on the door and arrested me.

> How did this affect him/the children/her? What is he realising when he looks at that?

5. What I would have liked to have done

> Positive self-talk

What I would like to have done: Apologised for not pre-planning my night out with her. said I understood why she was mad at me. reassured her I love her. not this other woman. tried to make up for it by offering her a night out while I babysit.

1. HOW IT STARTED

Remind yourself of Chapter 3.1. Ask the client to guess some of Carl's sore points and signals. Then show Carl's own answer and go on to complete this stage for your client's own storyboard.

2. JUST BEFORE THE ABUSE

Show your client the blank iceberg (it might be more useful to photocopy this on a sheet of A3 paper). Explain that people are a bit like icebergs in that you only see a small part of them (their words and actions). Most of what is important can't be seen and happens 'beneath the surface'.

Get your client to help you to fill in an iceberg for Carl. In the top section of the iceberg, above the surface of the water, fill out details of Carl's behaviour – his abusive actions and words. You can ask the client to imagine what Carl said and did in the build-up to being violent to Pat. Under the surface you will guess at some of Carl's feelings, thoughts and beliefs during the argument.

Then show them Carl's own attempt at the iceberg:

Note in particular the powerful emotions (in black) that usually drive the abuse and do get expressed, and the vulnerable emotions (in grey) that tend to get filtered out and remain unexpressed (such as fear or shame).

What effect did this negative self-talk have on the way Carl was feeling at the time? And what effects did his feelings have on his self-talk?

You can also briefly discuss Carl's beliefs, expectations and fears. You could discuss whether these are accurate or reasonable.

Now, draw another empty iceberg and look together at your client's own picture of 'just before' the incident. Then help them fill out the iceberg for their own incident.

3. DURING THE ABUSE

Show Carl's picture. Ask your client how Pat might have felt in this scene, and what he thinks Carl was saying or shouting during the abuse. Also ask how Ali might have felt if he'd woken up to hear this. Then show your client Carl's responses to these questions.

Now ask your client to add in their guess as to how the children and their partner felt in their own scenario.

4. THE AFTERMATH

Show Carl's picture of the aftermath. Ask what might have been the impacts on Carl, on Ali and on Pat. Then show Carl's own answer.

Ask your client to fill out the impacts on their own picture of the aftermath. Ask:

When you look at all this, what are you realising?

Give your client time to think about this and to answer with as much consideration and depth as they can. If they show remorse here, empathise with the painfulness of these realisations and praise them for their honesty and courage (where relevant) in doing this work.

5. WHAT I WOULD HAVE LIKED TO HAVE DONE

Show your client Carl's picture of what he wished he could have done (Carl has described this as what his 'ideal me' would have done).

Then ask your client what kinds of things Carl would have had to tell himself or think about to make himself behave in this way.

Show Carl's version of the self-talk he'd have needed, illustrated on the following page. Note that some of it is verbal but some is pictorial – he found it helpful to hold in mind an image of his child being scared by the violence, and an image of Pat at a moment when he'd felt really loving towards her.

Finally, ask your client to sketch what they'd like to have done differently and to detail the self-talk they'd have needed to do this.

INFORMATION SHEET 3.5.1

Carl's storyboard

Stage	How to work with this stage

1. How it started

How it started: she was asking me loads of questions about where I'd been and who was there.

→ Sore points and signals of build-up

2. Just before the abuse

Just before: we had argued for a while – we were in the living room... she stood up and swore at me...

→ Iceberg

3. During the abuse

What did he do/say? How did she feel? Let's imagine the kids heard this – how would they have felt?

During: I punched her back onto the sofa and went on hitting her. I got her one time on the face and then 3 or 4 times on the back and shoulder.

4. The aftermath

How did this affect him/ the children/ her? What is he realising when he looks at that?

The aftermath: Someone must have called the police – they banged on the door and arrested me.

5. What I would have liked to have done

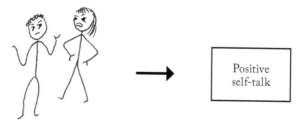

Positive self-talk

What I would like to have done: Apologised for not pre-planning my night out with her, said I understood why she was mad at me, reassured her I love her, not this other woman, tried to make up for it by offering her a night out while I babysit.

TASK SHEET 3.5.2

Carl's storyboard

1. How it started – Sore points and signals

<u>Sore points</u>

- It was late
- I was tired
- I'd been drinking
- Being questioned about where I've been
- Feeling 'caught out' (I know she wouldn't like who I've been out with)

<u>Signals</u>

- Physical – heating up, increased heart rate, tense jaw and shoulders.
- Behaviour – getting louder, gesticulating, frowning, glaring, pacing about.

2. Just before the Abuse – Carl's iceberg

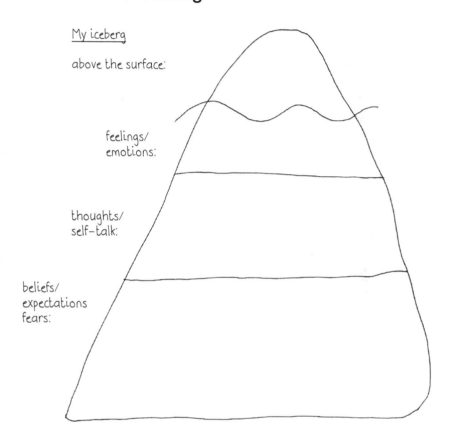

My iceberg

above the surface:

feelings/ emotions:

thoughts/ self-talk:

beliefs/ expectations fears:

2. Just before the Abuse
– Carl's iceberg

My iceberg

above the surface:

Shaking – calling her nosy, jealous, paranoid – standing over her

feelings/ emotions:

angry guilty trapped annoyed cornered punishing enraged controlled

thoughts/ self-talk:

you're a fxxxing lunatic! Get out of my face! Control-freak–what's wrong with you? You want to rule my life. I'm not a fxxxing child. How dare you swear at me! You paranoid bitch!

beliefs/ expectations fears:

She should not ask about my whereabouts. Let me stay out as long and as late as I want with whoever I want. Not swear at me or front up to me. Not make me feel bad or guilty if... then... If I have to check in with my partner then I am emascalated and infantilised. If I can't go out when and where I want I will look like a dick. If I am more direct about who and where I want to go she will complain. Worst fear – I will be under her thumb, lose my friends, lose all autonomy.

3. During the Abuse – Empathy

If our little one had heard he <u>would've</u> felt confused, terrified, scared, unsafe, helpsell, frozen

What she <u>might've</u> felt
shocked, terrified, pain, powerless, weak, helpless

<u>What I said:</u>

Don't you dare fuxxxing swear at me! Go on – swear at me now you bitch!

<u>What I did:</u>
I punched her hard to the head – she got a black eye. Then she covered her face so I thumped her 4 times – twice on the back and twice on the top of her arm – both were bruised

During: I punched her back onto the sofa and went on hitting her – I got her one time on the face and then 3 or 4 times on the back and shoulder.

4. The Aftermath – Impacts

Impacts on her:
hurt – physically and
emotionally.
Alone, ashamed.
Social care involved
torn (wanting the relationship
but angry)
Depressed, unloved

impacts on me:
Ashamed
restricted contact with
child – social care involved
held overnight in cell
loss of home
damage to relationship

impacts on child
confusion
loss of daddy
scared of daddy
mummy so sad
Police big and scary
very insecure
involvement
with childrens
social care

4. The aftermath: Someone must have called
the police – they banged on the door and
arrested me.

5. What I would have like to have done – Positive self talk

Ideal me

Apologise
reassure,
empathise,
make amends –
'Sorry – I'm not surprised
you're angry – You've
nothing to be insecure about
I love you   I'll make it up'

Self-talk:

She's just worried about
where I've been,
she's insecure
– it's a sign she cares about me.
It would be no big deal to send a text.

I don't want to be a scary nasty dad
like my dad was

Remember little Ali.

Remember this is the
woman I love.

Building Awareness of the Impacts of Domestic Violence

As a professional involved with a family where domestic violence is a child protection concern, you will be acutely aware of the potential impacts on the child of growing up with conflict and violence, and of the effect of persistent abuse on the victim's self-esteem and capacity as a parent. However, when you first meet them, the person using the violence is most likely to be shutting out any awareness they have of the impact of their actions, either by blaming others or minimising the seriousness of what is going on. If they are to become a more responsible partner and parent, it is crucial that they develop awareness of the impacts of domestic violence. However, we would recommend that when embarking on this work you do it in this order:

1. impacts on the perpetrator
2. impacts on the children
3. impacts on the adult victim.

Get that order wrong and you'll very likely come up against a wall of shame-driven denial and defensiveness.

Clients are also often feeling angry and resentful towards their partners when you first meet with them, and just aren't ready to try to put themselves in their partner's shoes. Get this order right though, and you will find that step 1 does a lot of the work that allows you to move onwards to steps 2 and 3.

1. Impacts on the perpetrator

The simplest way to look at the impacts on the perpetrator is to fill out a 'costs–benefits grid' with them (see Task Sheet 3.6.1).

When you ask a mum why she shouted at or smacked her child (at least in contexts where that is still acceptable) she's likely to tell you clearly that she was teaching them a lesson and she'll have little hesitation explaining what the lesson was – for example, to teach him not to slam doors or pick on his sister. Because domestic abuse is not seen as widely acceptable, the sense in which it is an attempt to 'discipline' an intimate to change their behaviour often gets mystified and lost.

As a result, when you do the costs–benefits grid, you may need to explore the benefits of violence and abuse in terms of the perpetrator getting their own way. Examples might be getting the victim to shut up, not talk to other men, avoid her family, stop criticising his drinking, etc.

Additionally, include the emotional benefits. Ask:

If you hadn't shouted and used violence then, and you just had to put up with the situation, what feelings might you have had?

Avoidance of painful feelings of powerlessness and vulnerability is usually at least a part of the benefit of using violence and abuse.

Ask your client about the practical costs of violence and abuse, such as social services involvement and loss of housing. There may also be less tangible impacts on relationships with family and friends who know a bit about what has happened. Are there people who they still fear knowing about what they did? How does that affect these relationships? Spend a good bit of time asking about any negative emotional impacts on the perpetrator – if they mention guilt and shame, find out when they felt worst and what they felt worst about.

Paradoxically, it's quite motivational to help your client to acknowledge their resistance to change. Many people have this – we just don't want to feel forced or manipulated and we often fear a loss of identity in changing lifelong ways of being.

Finally, include the possible benefits of changing: both for your client's self-esteem and for their relationships, not only to the victim, but to extended family, community and most of all to their children. Don't try and stack the odds on either side; simply acknowledge that your client faces a conflict – that change will be hard but the benefits could be substantial.

2. Impacts on the children

Once you've given adequate time to the perpetrator, it will be much easier to move on to the impacts on others. Since the iceberg analogy has already been introduced, it should be simple to return to it here. Remind your client that the iceberg is a useful metaphor for a person because most of what goes on is under the surface. Have your client draw an iceberg like the one on the next page.

Ask your client what their child shows on the surface when Mum and Dad fight. What is visible in terms of their actions and feelings? Draw or write this into the visible section of the iceberg.

Remind them that as children there are a lot of things that go on inside us that we never tell our parents. There are things that we sense shouldn't be spoken about, including things about the parents themselves.

Ask your client what their fears are about what their own child doesn't show, and what lies underneath the surface. Draw or write this into the submerged section of the iceberg.

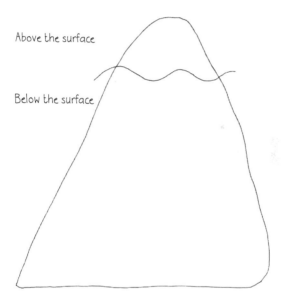

Comment on what you see in the parent's reaction to doing this exercise – for example:

As you look at that iceberg, I see your body language is a bit closed and you look uncomfortable.

Quickly sketch another iceberg and write what you see above the surface for the parent – then pass it over to them and ask them:

I wonder what is going on beneath the surface for you as you look at your child's iceberg.

3. Impacts on the adult victim

Ask your client if they feel willing and able to explore the impacts of the violence and abuse on their partner. Acknowledge that this is tricky to do and that sometimes anger and resentment can get in the way of us doing this with any honesty. Be clear that there's no point at all in doing it dishonestly – and check again that they feel ready to go ahead. This will allow you to set about filling out the grid 'Impacts on My Partner' (Task Sheet 3.6.2).

Wherever your client struggles for empathy you can ask:

What do you guess your partner might say if they were here answering these questions for themselves?

If they really struggle, you could use Information Sheet 3.6.1 – a list of impacts put together by women living with domestic violence. Ask whether and which of these might relate to the impacts on the adult victim in this family.

TASK SHEET 3.6.1

Impact on Me:
Costs and Benefits

Costs of continuing abuse and violence	Benefits of continuing abuse and violence
Costs of changing and stopping abuse	Benefits of changing and stopping abuse

TASK SHEET 3.6.2

Impacts on My Partner

The physical/health effects of domestic violence on victims	The emotional effects of domestic violence on victims
The effects of domestic violence for victims' relationships with the perpetrator	The effects on her ability to manage work and day-to-day tasks
The effects on her social and family relationships	The effects on her relationship with her children

INFORMATION SHEET 3.6.1

How Domestic Abuse Affected Us

There were injuries like:
Stiffness
Soreness
Aching
Bruising
Headaches
Cuts
Black eyes
Wounds
Hair pulled out
Broken ribs
Broken limbs

We also had:
Stress
Tension all the time
Difficulty sleeping
Exhaustion
Depression
Panic attacks
Palpitations
Eating disorders

And we became increasingly:
Obsessive
Neurotic
Compulsive
Self-harming
Suicidal

Some of us found:
Our periods stopped
We caught STDs from our partners
We got vaginismus
Felt physically sick

It made us feel:
Stressed
Scared
Damaged
Drained
Terrified
Worthless
Lost
Jumpy
That everything was too much
Confused
Insecure
That we couldn't go on
Alone
Unconfident
That we were going under
Hurt
Hard
Suicidal
Stuck
Useless
Frozen
Ashamed
Hemmed in
Unloved
Suspicious
Guilty
Nervous
Unlovable
Suffocated
Weak
Untrusting
Vulnerable
Ugly
Depressed
Too fat
Too thin
Crazy
Paranoid
Angry
Stupid
Betrayed
Humiliated

Like we had:
No energy
No space
No time
No control
We started to use:
Alcohol
Drugs
Anything to cope

It affected our work and day-to-day tasks – we started to:
Lose concentration
Take lots of sick days
Get things wrong
Become unreliable
Arrive late

As a result some of us began to:
Feel we couldn't manage the job
Feel we shouldn't be working at all
Run out of lies
Withdraw from colleagues
Become more isolated

We struggled with:
Getting out of bed in the morning
Washing
Dressing
Shopping
Eating

It affected things with our partners – we ended up:
Walking on egg shells
Trying to pacify them
Agreeing with them to stay safe
Focusing on them all the time and trying to figure out their moods
Hiding things from them
Being quiet and not sharing things with them
Not saying what we wanted to say
Lying to protect our children or ourselves
Losing sight of the person we loved
Feeling confused that we still cared
Being distant and withdrawn
Having outbursts of anger at them
Losing all sexual feelings for them
Having sex with them to improve their mood

It affected our social and family relationships:
We felt embarrassed
We ended up not wanting to go out
We felt stupid for putting up with it
We got nervous about who we talked to
We feared other people would know
Our friends and families divided and took sides
We feared they'd judge us
He threatened or hurt our family and friends
Either we didn't talk to them about the violence…
(Then we became more isolated and withdrawn)
Or we did talk to them… (Then they got frustrated with us for staying)
We felt caught between a rock and a hard place
He checked our phone bills or listened to our calls

We ended up having to defend our man
We felt self-conscious when he was there
We lost friends and family
We felt as if we were letting everyone down
He put us down in front of friends...
or was moody or rude when they came round...
then they stopped coming round
We didn't want to see anyone and we didn't want anyone to see us
We ended up alone
We ended up isolated
We felt watched, checked up on, monitored...
and we ended up monitoring ourselves so as not to get caught out

It affected our relationships with our children:
We were labelled as bad mothers
We felt as if they were judging us
We didn't feel like the adult
They blamed us
We felt that we hadn't got the energy for them
We felt bad for being down around them
We felt guilty to them for staying
Social services held us responsible
We felt guilty to them for leaving
They talked to us and treated us as he did

We feared that we were burdening the children if we showed our feelings...
They began to play up to us
...or we felt that we couldn't let our feelings out in front of them...
then we became withdrawn and unavailable
We could see the effects of the abuse on the children, and we felt inadequate, helpless, guilty
We were inconsistent with them
We felt as if we couldn't control ourselves
We couldn't control them

From K. Iwi and J. Todd (2000) *Working Towards Safety: A Guide to Domestic Violence Intervention Work*, Domestic Violence Intervention Project, London, UK.

CHAPTER 3.7

Conflict Resolution

Note: whilst this work can be done with the client alone to encourage them to take their partner's perspective in disputes, it may not be appropriate or possible to encourage them to put it into action with their partners if risk is high – the worker will need to judge from their knowledge of the situation in the family.

It's all very well to help someone to acknowledge their abusive behaviour and to motivate them to want to change – but it's important to enable them to go further than just taking time out whenever they feel angry. Even if they're going on to do a perpetrator programme, it can be empowering and motivational for them to learn some respectful and healthy ways to deal with conflict in their relationship at this early stage.

Go through and fill out Task Sheet 3.7.1 with your client, using the information from this to drive a discussion about what they could change in the way they approach arguments and disagreements. Ask your client if they are willing to work on some of these skills in the coming week whenever they are 'in conflict' – with their partner, professionals or others. Remember to check back on how it has gone.

It can be helpful to begin some practice right away in the sessions with you, where you are on hand to model the desired behaviour and to monitor and steer your client's efforts. An effective technique for developing listening and communication skills is 'checking back' between you whenever even a slight conflict arises in your work. This will be most effective if you have explicitly gained their full agreement and understanding upfront – it won't work well if you raise it for the first time in the midst of a heated discussion. Essentially, when things begin to feel difficult in the conversation, or either of you feels you're not being heard, you can simply say, 'Let's check back.' From then, one of you speaks and the other must check back what they heard, staying with this until the speaker agrees they've got it, before taking the floor themselves. Checking back can help on two levels – both by helping them to absorb whatever point you might be making, while also teaching a technique for improving communication.

Improving our skills for listening in conflict is likely to lead to our hearing things we don't like and leave us with some uncomfortable emotions. It's best to pre-empt this by discussing with your client what feelings they are likely to end up with and asking them what they might tell themselves to help them deal with such feelings.

Finding solutions for specific conflicts

There's a technique for going in-depth into a particularly hot or frequently argued-over issue. When you learn of such arguments you can begin a three-step process to deconstruct and analyse these.

Step 1

Explore your client's perspective on the issue. Do this by asking them the following four questions (you might want to make use of Task Sheet 3.7.2):

1. *How do you feel about this issue?* It's important to let your client express the impact of this argument on them; equally important when it comes to the second step of this exercise is for them to try to step into their partner's shoes on this question.

2. *How do you think you came to this particular view (a different view to your partner) about this?* Ask your client to try to speak about themselves and their own history here and explain to you where their beliefs come from.

   This question is designed to help your client recognise the relativity of their perspective. Sometimes we assume that we feel strongly about something because we are simply 'more right and more rational' than our partner. In fact, rather than some objective rationality being the *basis* for our views, we have mostly come to these views based on a mixture of personality, temperament, life history and experience – and are generally only employing our rationality to justify and back them up. It can help to recognise that many of our beliefs – especially about relationships – are subjective, culturally constructed and hatched within the context of our own very particular, and often rather strange, families of origin.

3. *In the argument with your partner, what needs of yours are not being met?* Ideally, go beyond your client's wants – such as 'I want to be able to go out' – and

seek the deeper need. If this remains a very superficial discussion, you might want to look together at the list underlying human needs on Information Sheet 3.7.1 at the end of the chapter to see if any fit.

4. *If you can't get your way in this argument, and perhaps you never get your way on this issue, what is your worst fear?* Often, our arguments are almost 'symptoms' of deeper issues – until we look at the worst fears (which often reveal where the real heat is coming from) we may end up dealing with endless skirmishes without ever addressing the root cause.

Step 2

Explore the other person's perspective. Between you, you are going to guess at what their partner's answers to the same questions would be. If they're willing, you can get your client to sit in a different seat and speak as their partner. If that seems a bit too much like 'role play' then you can simply ask them, 'What would your partner say to that?'

Step 3

Consolidate this learning. Discuss with your client whether it makes a difference to step into their partner's shoes in this way. Ask them if they can think of solutions that seem fair, realistic and have at least taken care of both parties' underlying needs and worst fears. Feel free to help them out with this – making suggestions for other options and helping them to increase the range of possible solutions open to them without pushing them to agreeing to do something they won't follow through with.

Ask your client what they want to remember from this exercise. It's a technique you can use again as you hear about new issues coming up in the relationship and is good practice for their being able to tackle conflicts more constructively as they arise.

TASK SHEET 3.7.1

Conflict Resolution

Rate yourself from 1 to 10 (where 1 is 'I find this very difficult' and 10 is 'I find this very easy') on the following conflict reduction/resolution skills:

Listening even when angry	
Not seeking to blame or put down the other person in argument	
Keeping a calm demeanour – tone of voice/body language	
Weighing up criticisms against you fairly	
Making honest apologies when appropriate – without a 'tit-for-tat' clause	
Being the one to offer the 'olive branch' and set about making peace, even if you feel you were 'in the right'	
Being caring even when you don't feel good	

Conflict resolution skills	
Have you ever managed to deal with a conflict in a way you felt really good about? What did you do?	
Have you known anyone who was particularly good at resolving this sort of conflict? How did they do it?	
How would you like someone to respond to you in a conflict?	
How do you know you're being listened to and heard?	

Kate Iwi and Chris Newman © 2015

Finding Solutions for Specific Conflicts

What is the conflict or issue you're examining?	
Your view	
How do you feel about this issue?	
How do you think you came to this particular view (a different view to your partner) about this?	
In the argument with your partner, what underlying needs of yours are not being met? (It may help to look at the Information Sheet 3.7.1.)	

If you can't get your way in this argument, and perhaps you never get your way on this issue, what is your worst fear?	

Your partner's view	
How does your partner feel about this issue?	
How do you think s/he came to this particular view (a different view to your own) about this?	
What underlying needs of his or hers do you think are not being met?	
If your partner can't get their way in this argument, and perhaps never gets their way on this issue, what is their worst fear?	

Examples of Underlying Human Needs

Connection

acceptance
affection
appreciation
belonging
cooperation
communication
closeness
community
companionship
compassion
consideration
consistency
empathy
inclusion
intimacy
love
mutuality
nurturing
respect/self-respect
safety
security
stability
support
to know and be known
to see and be seen
to understand and be understood
trust
warmth

Meaning

awareness
celebration of life
challenge
clarity
competence
consciousness
contribution
creativity
discovery
efficacy
effectiveness
growth
hope
learning
mourning
participation
purpose
self-expression
stimulation
to matter
understanding

Peace

beauty
communion
ease
equality
harmony
inspiration
order

Physical wellbeing

air
food
movement/exercise
rest/sleep
sexual expression
safety
shelter
touch
water

Autonomy

choice
freedom
independence
space
spontaneity

Honesty

authenticity
integrity
presence

Play

joy
humour

4 – WHAT NEXT?

CHAPTER 4.1

Referring Onwards

Assuming you've managed to engage your client and set them off along the path towards change, you're going to want to ensure that they continue along that route – that they capitalise on and consolidate the work they've begun with you.

Domestic violence perpetrator programmes

The best-fit service for referring them on will most likely be a domestic violence perpetrator programme. You can find the options available to you locally by contacting Respect,[1] the UK membership association for domestic violence perpetrator programmes and associated support services.

Respect run two helplines:

- *Respect Phoneline*: 0808 802 4040, www.respectphoneline.org.uk – for domestic violence perpetrators and professionals who would like further information about services for those

---

1   www.respect.uk.net

using violence/abuse in their intimate partner
relationships

- Men's Advice Line: Freephone 0808 801 0327
www.mensadviceline.org.uk – for men
experiencing domestic violence.

Respect-accredited perpetrator programmes are long – from
24 weeks upwards – and recognise that to achieve lasting
changes there is a need to go further than the interventions
you can find in this handbook and address deep-seated
belief systems and/or emotional developmental legacies
that underlie the anger and use of violence.

> Outcome studies suggest that violence/abuse
> elimination occurs from reconstructing clients'
> entrenched belief systems [...] and enhancing victim
> empathy and co-operative decision-making rather
> than from the management or control of anger.
> (Healey, Smith and O'Sullivan 1998)

Perpetrator programmes are by no means watertight, and
there is a lot of controversy in the research literature about
their effectiveness. However, recent reviews indicate that
they have a stronger evidence base than other interventions.[2]
In particular, there is strong evidence for the effectiveness
of the predominant cognitive behavioural approach which
underpins most programmes.

What's key about Respect-accredited programmes
is that they take into account the safety implications for
partners when an abuser sets out on a programme, for the
following reasons:

- The fact that he is on a programme may mean
that the victim has unrealistic expectations of her

---

2 See E. Gondolf (2011, 2012).

own and her children's safety. People tend to put their trust in professionals, so they assume that if their partner is on a programme, they are going to change.

- These unfounded expectations (as it is not possible to predict at the outset whether the abuser will change) extend to professionals – such as family court judges.

- The fact that her abuser is in some form of counselling has a significant influence over a woman's decision to return to her abusive partner (Scott 2004).

Current best practice guidelines therefore require that perpetrator programmes offer support services which help to counter these expectations and impacts.

However, for a number of reasons you may find it hard to refer your client into such a programme. Most often this will be because there's a lack of local resources or the funding to pay for a place. In those cases you might be tempted to use alternatives. Alternative types of intervention are highly controversial, and if you're considering one then you should do so with your eyes wide open to the reasons for this.

A note of caution for social workers

As mentioned in Chapter 1.1 recent changes to the child protection system in England and Wales set a strict 26-week deadline for care proceedings to finish. As a result, parents now have much less time to demonstrate change once proceedings have started. Because programme referrals rarely take place at the start of proceedings, this means that it is unlikely that there will be time for the abusive partner to fully demonstrate their capacity to change, and for programme staff and those making assessments of change in risk to assess treatment outcome.

When considering a behaviour change programme as a way of managing risk, practitioners should build into their thinking from the outset the fact that not all perpetrators of abuse change due to a programme, and of those who do make changes, some will not change enough to ensure the safety of their ex-partners and children. There is no accurate way to predict whether the programme will prove effective with any given client. Although motivation to change seems to be an important factor in successful programme outcomes, *it cannot be assumed that the risk has decreased simply because a client is attending or has completed a programme.* Practitioners should therefore:

- check that the programme is suitable, and that there is evidence that this kind of programme will work cooperatively with other agencies involved in the case

- request that the agency providing the programme receive full details of the risk concerns which have given rise to the referral

- request interim reports on participation and progress

- reassess the risk upon completion of a programme.

Practitioners should be aware of the risk that a person may misuse attendance on a treatment programme to manipulate others. For example, some clients may use private law proceedings to further pursue their ex-partners. This kind of client may have the determination to sit through a long programme with little chance that any meaningful change will take place.

Treatment suitability

What should you be looking for to determine whether a referral to a behaviour change programme is likely to reduce the risk and help your client change?

- Some acknowledgement that violence and abuse is a problem for them. A degree of minimisation is quite normal, and reduction in minimisation can be regarded as a treatment aim rather than a prerequisite. However, if a person works with you over a number of weeks on the material presented in this book, and they are still denying the bulk of concerns about the abusive behaviour which led to the referral, then you will need to question whether he or she is suitable for a programme.

- Willingness to focus on changing their own behaviour, rather than relying on their partner to act differently.

- In their work with you, a capacity to reflect on their behaviour, and to focus on and identify thinking patterns and emotional states that take place during abusive episodes.

- A sense that they want to change for the sake of their child.

- Capacity to benefit from the programme. Consider cognitive abilities and mental health problems here.

- Capacity to be sober during sessions. If a person's substance abuse problem means that they are unlikely to be able to be sober during sessions – this usually means being able to abstain for 24 hours before sessions – then they are unlikely to benefit.

Anger management

Let's not malign anger management – substantial elements of the work in this book, and at the start of most DV perpetrator programmes, could come under the title of 'anger management'. Indeed, the signals and self-talk chapter of this book is largely *about* anger management.

However, teaching anger management techniques alone is only likely to go part of the way to helping someone to stop abusing an intimate partner. Anger management is usually a short-term, skills-based intervention based upon the idea that the client has difficulty controlling anger.

The instrumentality of domestic violence is not captured by most anger management work, nor the relevance of entitlement, beliefs and expectations. The impact of insecure attachment styles that may predispose people to go to great lengths to control the distance of intimacy between themselves and their partners – the proprietorial, jealous obsessions some people have that lead them to want to keep their partners incredibly close, and the avoidant, invaded 'get out of my face' rages that lead others to push their partners away – will not be touched by short-term interventions. Furthermore, empathy and love for the victim and children aren't mobilised by anger management interventions – though these may be far and away the strongest motivation for change. Lastly, most anger management interventions do not provide partner support, which means they have no mechanism to counter the risk of creating unsafe and unrealistic expectations in the non-abusive partner.

Couples work/mediation

Another intervention often sought to resolve DV is couples work or mediation. However, in couples work:

- the victim is unlikely to feel confident enough to speak freely – this will exacerbate the power imbalance

- if s/he does speak freely, they may be punished later with physical violence or other abuse for speaking out of turn

- the implication is that both people have some responsibility for the violence, which may exacerbate self-blame and the idea that if the victim doesn't change then the perpetrator is justified in their abuse.

Violence exists and persists in close relationships partly due to a focus on the victim's behaviour and how it makes the perpetrator feel. A shift needs to happen so that the focus turns to the perpetrator's behaviour and how this affects the victim. This is not always achieved in couples work, which traditionally strives towards a balance of responsibility for any given problem.

This is not to say that couples work cannot ever take place where there has been violence in the relationship. Because violence can be employed to stop and 'win' arguments, the underlying problems in the relationship often come to the fore when the violence ceases (not least the victim's previously suppressed anger at how they have been treated). Such issues can be very effectively explored in a couples counselling setting (Respect 2008). However, this is complex work and cannot take place where one partner still fears the other. In addition, most agencies which have piloted couples work with domestic abuse have used extensive screening interviews to ensure that they include couples with only 'low levels' of violence (Gondolf 2011).

Relate and Respect have developed some guidelines for when couples work is and is not appropriate in cases where there has been domestic violence.[3] These guidelines indicate that if a thorough, structured assessment interview with each partner (seen individually) reveals that there is no current abuse, coercion or threat (a possible guideline might be one year since the last serious violence or abusive incident) and each partner is asking to be seen together, then couples counselling may be offered. However, because violence and abuse can be cyclical in nature, ongoing assessment should be built in to the work, and there should be a continued focus on safety.

Relate also emphasise that any work with couples where there is ongoing domestic abuse should be conducted within a context of a community network of care rather than in a counselling 'bubble'. So a multi-agency approach is crucial.

Considerations for workers

It should also be noted that working together on difficult issues over a number of weeks will inevitably intensify the relationship between client and worker. This has an advantage but also risks.

The *advantage* is that a positive working alliance can be a powerful motivator for change. The *risks* are perhaps an increased danger of losing objectivity and being drawn into the world view of the client you are working with. Regular supervision and discussion with other workers (especially with those working with his or her partner) will help to counter this. With some offenders, the individual setting may also leave workers more vulnerable to direct or subtle forms of abuse and manipulation. Again, procedures should

---

3   See Owen (2010) Respect (2008) Repect's guidelines are available at www.respect.uk.net.

be set in place, via peer and formal supervision, to counter this.

Lastly, one of the more mundane pitfalls of working individually is that workers may find themselves spending large parts of each session in general discussions of problems which are at best only marginally related to the purpose of the programme. Remember that whilst one of the advantages of individual work is that you can be responsive and work with issues which are current, you have a limited number of sessions in which to:

- assess 'treatment viability'

- provide a focused piece of work, in which you can set in place some risk-reduction strategies for your client and help him or her develop hope for change.

References

Gondolf, E. (2011) 'The weak evidence for batterer program alternatives.' *Aggression and Violent Behavior 16*, 347–353.

Gondolf, E. (2012) *The Future of Batterer Intervention Programs*. Boston: Northeastern University Press.

Healey, K., Smith, S. and O'Sullivan, C. (1998) *Batterer Intervention: Program Approaches and Criminal Justice Strategies*. Washington, DC: US Department of Justice Office of Justice Programs, National Institute of Justice.

Owen, R.E. (2010) 'Bridging to change: Relate's domestic violence and abuse responsive model.' *Safe 32*, Winter.

Respect (2008) *Indicators for Referral to Couples Counselling Following Domestic Violence Prevention Programme Attendance*. London: Respect.

Scott, K. (2004) *Do Batterer Intervention Programs Work? Professional Education for Community Practitioners*. Technical Paper Series, User-Report 2004:01.

INDEX